W0081409

Night Swimming

How to Swim Through the Darkness

DISCLAIMER

This book is intended solely for informational and inspirational purposes. It is based on the author's personal experiences and opinions and should not be considered professional advice, training or a substitute for consulting qualified and certified experts.

The activities described in this book, including night swimming and other water-based practices, involve inherent risks and dangers, including but not limited to injury, illness, drowning or death. The author is an experienced night swimmer and has undertaken years of careful research and training in order to prepare him to undertake the activities described in this book. Readers are strongly advised to:

• Evaluate their physical and mental condition and seek medical advice before attempting any activities described.
• Consult certified professionals and local authorities for guidance on water safety and conditions.
• Research local conditions, including weather and water behaviour, and assess their suitability for any activity described.
• Use appropriate safety equipment and prepare thoroughly for all activities.

Environmental conditions, including water temperature, weather and currents, can vary greatly and may differ significantly from the author's experiences. Readers are solely responsible for determining their level of preparedness, acquiring necessary training and using appropriate safety equipment for any activity described.

The author and publisher disclaim all liability for injuries, losses, damages or deaths that may result from the use or misuse of the information in this book. By engaging in any activities described, readers explicitly assume all risks, responsibilities and consequences for their actions.

This book is provided "as is", without any guarantees or assurances of safety, accuracy or suitability for individual circumstances. If in doubt, consult professional experts before undertaking any activity described.

Night Swimming

How to Swim Through the Darkness

Al Mennie

WATKINS

Night Swimming

by Al Mennie

This edition first published in the UK and USA in 2025 by
Watkins, an imprint of Watkins Media Limited
Unit 11, Shepperton House, 89-93 Shepperton Road
London, N1 3DF

enquiries@watkinspublishing.com

Design and typography copyright © Watkins Media Limited 2025
Text copyright © Al Mennie 2025

Al Mennie has asserted his right under the Copyright, Designs
and Patents Act 1988 to be identified as the author of this work.

All rights reserved.
No part of this book may be reproduced or utilized in any form
or by any means, electronic or mechanical,
without prior permission in writing from the Publishers.

1 2 3 4 5 6 7 8 9 10

Designed and typeset by JCS Publishing Services Ltd
Printed and bound by CPI Group (UK) Ltd, Croydon, CR0 4YY
Cover design and illustrations by Alice Claire Coleman
Commissioning Editor: Sophie Blackman

The manufacturer's authorised representative in the EU for product safety is:
eucomply OÜ - Pärnu mnt 139b-14, 11317 Tallinn, Estonia,
hello@eucompliancepartner.com, www.eucompliancepartner.com

A CIP record for this book is available from the British Library

ISBN: 978-1-78678-994-5 (Paperback)
ISBN: 978-1-78678-995-2 (eBook)

MIX
Paper | Supporting
responsible forestry
FSC
www.fsc.org   FSC® C013604

www.watkinspublishing.com

To my loving companion Blyton.

Through the moonlight and every dark tide,
we swim side-by-side.

CONTENTS

CHAPTER 1

WATER BORN

In the vast and unruly North Atlantic Ocean, each wave is unique. Formed by the clash of tides, the push of the wild wind and the determination of cold, deep currents, each wave carries the power of the elements that sculpted it. Just like these waves, each of us is a creation of many forces clashing in an unrepeatable blend of past and present, gifting us the energy to become the future. Just as the gales churn the water, yet a gentle breeze softens the texture, we are each the result of an infinite number of possibilities and variations in the elements. We each have unique strengths, a resilient ancestry and a sea of challenges all surging into one almighty wave in the ocean of humanity.

Grains of sand

Imagine life as a beach where each grain of sand has travelled a different path, through the deepest waters on earth, to form the wild and unique sculpture of a beautifully forged bay. This blend of grains is what makes us who we are. With each tide, the sea reforms the beach. Some of the sand is washed away, never to return, and at other times sand is pushed further ashore bringing even more dimensions to the beach. And that is just like the experiences that wash in and out of our life, each one altering us and sculpting us into a unique and beautiful individual.

We are not simply one of some 8 billion humans living on earth – we are forces of nature, a source of endless power and possibility, just like the waves of the ocean.

Anchored

My father had come to Northern Ireland, aged 16, with his mother after the sudden passing of his father. They had spent many summer holidays in the fishing port of Portavogie on the east coast, and so felt at home here after such a traumatic loss. My dad spent time on trawlers and no doubt found his love of fishing and the water around Portavogie. He met my mother here, tall with long blonde hair and a striking presence, who came from a red-brick, terraced street in East Belfast, Northern Ireland.

I was born in 1980 during a tumultuous era in Belfast. Gunfire and bombings were a common occurrence as communities and governments fought for control. On the night I was born, my mother lay across the back seat of the car while my father, a large, red-headed Scotsman, navigated military checkpoints en route to the hospital. The car was stopped multiple times by soldiers demanding to know why he was driving into the city, late on a winter's night. It was a troubled time in this country's history, but it sculpted resilience and tenacity in our population.

Maybe the harsh westerly winds and gigantic seas that continually test the toughness of our island have fostered a unique strength in the people, to withstand the darkest times of life.

We lived in the countryside among rolling hills, with lakes and a little stream nearby, but no sea. The sea was half an hour away by car and we would spend our weekends at various beaches and on boats and Dad would fish.

For as long as I can remember, I could fish, row a boat and swim. I can't recall the first times I did any of those, as they were woven so seamlessly into my early years. My young mind was immersed in the moment, all the while soaking up the knowledge the water was pouring into me.

I believe if we look to our childhood for what grabbed the attention of our young and curious minds, we can find where our souls are anchored and use that to prevent us becoming adrift in the sea of life. The skills around the water that were inherited from my father, and learned through experience, are what anchor me. They were my first teachings around the water, but it would be many years before I would understand their importance. I hold those skills dear and they provide me with grounding against the relentless push and pull of life.

My first day on a surfboard is etched in my mind. There was a wild November winter swell at Castlerock on the north coast of Ireland. A brisk offshore wind whisked the crest off the top of the waves as they crashed toward shore and white sand tumbled along the beach. My parents and our dog Scott watched as my brother Andrew and I attempted to surf.

I remember what a struggle it was to stand up as the waves surged ashore, throwing me and the board toward the beach. But it didn't scare me – I loved it! Maybe, at nine, I was naive to the power of the ocean, but I think being in and around the water a lot had instilled confidence in me. Every time I fell into the crashing surf, I popped back up, pulled my board back and tried again.

Eventually, the "me against the sea" attitude of thrashing my way through the surf grew into a more refined display of navigation through rip currents, lulls and undertows. The experience was a childhood lesson in perseverance that rewarded me with knowledge I couldn't learn any other way.

But this is Ireland: it is cold, wild and, at times, bleak. It is very different to surfing the Pacific shores, where surfers are tanned, wear shorts and the weather is pleasant. To be a surfer in 1980s Ireland required an unbreakable desire – we didn't have the good wetsuits and boards available today. While many other children played football, rugby, hurling, etc., I was one of very few interested in surfing.

Committed to the water

Just as the tide fills the bay, the sea began to swell into every nook and cranny of my being. I became obsessed with surfing, at times spending whole days in the water. I'd be in the surf before the sun rose, and I would often be walking the beach in the dark until I could no longer see the waves coming. My parents gave me two rules: I had to leave the water when the streetlights came on and I wasn't allowed to surf waves that were taller than me. However, if I didn't look ashore, I could argue that I didn't notice the lights were on, and the size of waves was impossible to measure anyway . . .

I discovered a film about the surfers who rode the big waves in Half Moon Bay, California, at a break known as "Mavericks". It mesmerized me to the point that I watched it hundreds of times. I dissected every frame of the wave breaking, using the pause button on the player, studying how the surfers expertly timed catching the waves. The dark menacing walls of water collapsing and exploding, as what appeared to be tiny superheroes slid down the face on gigantic surfboards, captivated me. I said out loud, "I want to do that one day, I want to ride one of those big waves."

Because we lived in the countryside, and I was too young to drive, I spent every evening thinking about how I could train to become a better surfer without being in the sea. I began to swim a kilometre (⅝ of a mile) every night after school. I swam a lot underwater, figuring it might be beneficial to my surfing if I could hold my breath if caught under by a wave. I'd thrust myself down below the surface, and with both feet push off the wall and into a torpedo shape to hydrodynamically flow through the water. I'd take purposeful strokes so as not to create drag, all the way across the pool. Without surfacing I'd turn underwater, place my feet on the wall and push off again. Holding onto my breath I'd keep swimming until I reached the wall again.

I became good enough at swimming to win a gala in school and good enough at surfing that by age 15 I had been selected for the Irish Surf Team.

However, my pool training lasted only until I could drive; as soon as I could, I took my swimming training into the sea. To be a good surfer I needed to know how to navigate through the waves, the erratic currents and the crashing surf, with, or without, a board. The technicalities of that interested me more than those of pool swimming. By 17, my training involved swimming the length of Castlerock beach, in all conditions, and then running back through the sand dunes.

From pool to sea

Transitioning my swimming out of the pool and into the sea made me confident as both a surfer and a swimmer. However, my swim stroke changed dramatically. Swimming efficiently in the pool meant face in the water and an elongated body and stroke. In the surf, swimming is very different. After a few facefuls of white water, I learned quickly to keep my head on a swivel! Swimming in the surf means being alert and aware. Swimming in a thick wetsuit meant there was much more buoyancy, so kicking legs wasn't as important. To this day I believe that, to be proficient in the water requires a similar approach to fostering any relationship – it takes time, attention and a desire to swim through both the roughest, and the calmest, of waters.

New depths

I competed for Ireland on several occasions, ranked well on the British Pro Surf Tour, and won many competitions and accolades along the way. But just as swimming and surfing felt like steps on my path through the water, I now wanted to ride waves as tall as houses. In my view, big wave surfers are the essence of what it is to be perfectly in tune with the environment. Big wave surfing happened in Hawaii and California – I believed that my flow through life to date had primed me for riding the North Atlantic waves.

I did not set out on a course of study, I didn't look to become certified by anyone – the sea provided the curriculum, presented me with challenges, and examined my understanding and retention of crucial information. There was no skipping modules or cheating.

I remember the first time I lost my board in big waves at Castlerock, leaving me among the surf, way out in the sea. I had no option but to dive off my board as the wave broke in front of me. Just like I'd practised in the swimming pool, I held my breath. But the contrast between calmly blowing all my air out and then getting a big clean fresh breath of air, to the reality of being faced with a crashing wave and no time to prepare is quite different! I learned quickly that the choppy water, the wind and the slight panic all made me feel like taking a big gulp of air was not a risk worth taking in the wild outdoors, with a big wave roaring toward me.

I closed my mouth and swam down, pushing my hands out into the dark, peat-stained water, to pull me below the surface. The wave rumbled overhead but I was deep enough to not be hit too badly– until suddenly, the wave grabbed my board. Attached to it by my ankle leash, I felt the leash stretch, and then snap, as the board was taken by the wave. I was left suspended underwater, concerned for how many more waves there might be, now that I no longer had my board for buoyancy. I swam up for air and immediately felt very alone and vulnerable. I hadn't realized how much the board felt part of me in those conditions.

I swam toward the shore, using the flow of the broken wave to help carry me forward, constantly glancing behind for the next wave. My board had gone but I had a valuable lesson in using the water to my advantage. After the energy of the wave dissipated, smaller waves broke and helped wash me ashore. In the shallows I could see my board with the broken leash hanging off the back of it. Only then did I realize the other half was still attached to my ankle!

Stepping it up

On a beautiful summer evening, I sat in the garden with Dad talking about me feeling ready to surf Mavericks. He knew I had surfed lots of sizeable waves around Ireland, and in other parts of Europe, and he believed I was ready for the next stage.

The next evening, I got a phone call to tell me he had passed away, not long after swimming in the pool he had built for us at home. He was only 50 years old. That conversation about surfing was the last conversation we had. The last piece of support and guidance I'd ever receive from him.

I channelled all my grief into the water. I gave myself to the sea. I wanted it to sculpt me, sharpen the edges of my ability and fine-tune what it had already created in me. I spent the next six months training with razor-sharp focus. I devised my own training plan of surf swimming, weight-training, surfing and underwater rock-running (inspired by the Hawaiians, where they'd swim down to pick up a rock and run across the ocean floor, holding their breath).

With every stroke I swam in the wild Atlantic, I'd see every wave that washed over me as one in the Pacific at Mavericks. I'd imagine the turbulence, visualize the under-violence of 12-metre (40-foot) waves detonating over a submerged reef, and my mind would play flashbacks from the hours of videos I'd watched. In those days I was training for survival, less so performance. I was thinking of the sea from as many perspectives as possible, trying to prepare myself for the challenges ahead.

In the December after my father died, I achieved my dream of surfing the huge waves at Mavericks. In doing so, I learned that I was capable. It also proved to be a significant point in my life, diverting the flow to the next stage: to go in hunt of uncharted waves and break new ground in big wave surfing in Ireland. Surfing became an all-consuming pursuit that distracted from my loss.

A change of tide

Tall, black basalt, from ancient lava flows, tower over the golden sands at Castlerock. A little cove toward the western end of the beach is carved into the rock below the cliff. It was the ideal spot to build castles, tunnels and boats in the sand. So many childhood memories and Dad's photographs, which blend together so that I can no longer tell what I remember and what I know only from the family albums.

As I walk through the cove on a grey winter's day, I realize that, over the past 40 years, the sea has continued to thrash, smash, hammer and caress that little cove. Every piece of rock and sand ever-so-slightly changed by the sea in that time. Some rocks are unrecognizable, others don't look much different. In the past 40 years, the same waters have also sculpted me. From those days when I played on the beach as a little boy, to today, the sea and sand have, in many ways, sculpted who I am. This coastline has witnessed me grow through all eras of my life, just as I have watched it.

I believe we are part of this planet. Just as the rocks, the sea and the sand form the elements upon which we live, we are as much a part of nature as they are. While our individual stories may differ, we have all been sculpted by our surroundings and the environment in which we spend our days. The years of staying connected to the sea and allowing it to sculpt my journey gave me tools for every eventuality I may face, both in the water, and in life. In this book I share many of those with you, so you too can benefit from the power of the water and develop your own personal connection to it.

When I began night swimming in 2020, it gave me a new view of a world I didn't think I could know any better. Just as I have learned about the water since I was a child, I started yet another stage of learning, but in a much more personal way. Night swimming has shone light into my knowledge of the sea, but also of myself. In this book, I will pass that knowledge on to you. I hope that if you ever try to see your world from a different vantage point, or take up swimming or night swimming, that this book is a companion on your journey.

A greater purpose

I have always used the lessons I've taken from my experiences in the sea to give back. I've seen my time with the sea as a privilege – to have built such a deep relationship with the natural world. Where possible, I've attempted to turn that into positivity for others.

In my career, I have written around the topics of confidence, fear, loss and many other things that we struggle with as humans. I do not pertain to have all the answers, but there have been many times in my life where I have wished that someone was there to help and guide me through the darkest waters of my life, when in reality, I faced many alone. For that reason, I will always put my experiences out there in the hope that someone else may take something from them, to help others navigate their own way through life.

During the lockdowns, I wondered whether I'd learned something that might make a difference to others. The sea surely did not sculpt me for the sole purpose of riding waves and taking risks with my life for personal gain or a trophy. I felt there was more to it, so I began a campaign, Swim Through Darkness, that I hoped might make a difference to the mental health struggles being faced by an increasing number of people. Swim Through Darkness was born out of the hope that my night swimming might, in some way, bring hope to people struggling to keep their head above water.

CHAPTER 2
NIGHT BECOMES LIGHT

I was blinded by darkness long after sundown, suspended in the turbulence of storm-driven waves. The water spun, twisting and spiralling around and around until it released me. The roar of wild winter surf filled my ears as I tore through the surface. Once I was sure where I faced, I opened my lungs and drew a breath before the next wave bore down. My senses filled by the raging North Atlantic as it rumbled overhead. But I wasn't scared. No panic. Just completely at ease and at peace with this beautiful, chaotic moment in time.

Getting into the flow

Swimming at night takes outdoor swimming to another level, and to consider it requires dedication. But you don't have to swim out into the raging surf in the dark and cold for you to benefit from night swimming. The act of night swimming is not as blatant as simply swimming at night – it is much more. Both words "night" and "swimming" have meaning on a spectrum – with night, we assume it's dark, but it's not always pitch dark. With swimming, we don't always need to be in deep water, swimming like Olympians. You might not need to be any deeper into the water than having it gently wash around your knees and thighs; it is enough to simply close your eyes and feel the sea move and touch you as you stand in the shallows. So, if you wish to try night swimming, where do you start?

To do this safely requires much more than rushing down to the nearest water and jumping in. Begin by building up your experience of swimming in your local water by day, whether the sea, a lake or river. Then you can start small and do it to a level that feels safe for you. You may have intricate knowledge of your local lake or river, so your night swims will be very different from mine in the ocean, but it's all still night swimming. I've found night swimming to be transformative but it's important to approach it with the proper mindset and preparation. It's not just about the act of swimming, but about connecting with the environment in a meaningful way.

The simple act of being in or near the water after sundown is only part of what can become a lifestyle. I enjoy the process of constantly checking the weather and the sea state throughout the day, watching the tide rise and fall, and visualizing my time in the water after dark. The actual swimming is a small part of it all. It's a way of life, and I hope it can be the same for you too. The water demands that from us – there is no room for a lack of respect or underestimating the power it has to take you in an instant.

Flow state of mind

I sometimes wonder why I go out there. Why have I felt the need to constrict my senses so much so that I can barely see where I am swimming? Why do I swim out into the North Atlantic in every condition, from calm mysterious nights, to wild raging seas?

As I leave the perceived security of the streetlights behind, venturing out onto the vast sands of my local beach fills me with emotion. Excitement flows, nerves surface and fear threatens to ruin the whole endeavour. But, most of all, I feel like I'm entering another dimension as I walk further into the darkness and emptiness. Nothing is more awakening than the heavy darkness of a stormy night falling all around me, absorbing me.

As I walk out across the beach on those dark nights, the sea gets louder, and the dark gets darker. The voice of the sea hypnotizes me, quietly ushering the noise from daily life into empty corners of my mind. By the time I've reached the water's edge, I'm focused solely on that very moment.

The darkness conceals life's distractions, helping me slip into the elusive state where the mind and body flow together, creating the perfect connection between me and the environment. My senses bathe in the darkness, immersed in the sound of the water, the rush of waves and the bite of the cold.

According to Kendra Cherry of verywellmind.com, a "flow state" characteristic may be synchronization: "Flow allows certain regions of the brain to communicate with one another more effectively. While in a flow state, there may be an increase in activity in the frontal cortex, contributing to increased higher thinking."

Being in a flow state is regarded by many psychologists as promoting emotional regulation, fulfilment and happiness.

But the darkness and this flow state may also conceal danger. Brent Hogarth, a sports and clinical psychologist, explains that "flow may also elicit a sense of self control, dependence and risky behaviours with negative consequences."

Brent specifically references big wave surfing in an article, "Shining light on the dark side of flow-state," where he talks of research carried out on adventure athletes. He drew the conclusion that "flow may help high-flow-athletes and professionals develop greater self-mastery in order to reach their goals safely."

Mindfulness, in this same moment, may be what keeps us safe and from danger. There must be a balance between this magical flow state and mindfulness to allow us to safely immerse ourselves in the water after dark.

Life at the water's edge

Night swimming could be a dangerous thing to do if I did not have an intricate understanding of all the elements that may affect the water and me. Even with decades of experience and knowledge of my local waters, there is every chance, on any night, that I may not return. I could not be more aware of that. In my 40-odd years of swimming in these waters, the more I learn how insignificant my life is in the grand scheme of things. But I think that is part of the attraction. It's a reality check. It's a good thing to take a step away from my life for a moment and put it all into perspective. And if risks are identified through experience and knowledge, I believe they can be managed. If I don't learn how to safely remove myself from my ordinary life, then I don't grow as a person. I need to learn, experience, fall, and get back up, to develop as a human. I think night swimming provides me with that.

When I first started night swimming, I had a mixture of feelings about being in the sea and the surf after dark. As much as I wanted to do it, I experienced fear and uncertainty. I found it difficult to relax. I stayed in the relative safety of waist-deep water. I'd wade out into the water where the waves would rush at me from the dark and it was exciting, but I could still see to varying degrees.

It quickly became something I looked forward to all day. I wanted the sun to set, to go back out on the beach, to go a little bit further, to begin to swim, and venture a bit more into the dark. The darkness that came into life from the onset of the pandemic began to lift with night swimming.

I'd sit by my window overlooking the beach I've surfed and swam at all my life. As the tide rose and filled in between the rises of sand and rock, I'd see tiny changes in the water movement I'd not noticed before. Logs and sticks that were once immersed in the water's energy would be left on the beach as the tide dropped out. I'd watch little rip currents form and work their way back out to sea through the raging white froth. The sea was showing me intricate detail. As the chaos of modern life slowed, my connection to the sea deepened. I was noticing things I may have previously taken for granted or not considered relevant in my excitement to be out in the surf. To swim where the sea crashes, roars, pushes and pulls, required me to allow myself into a different head space. Instead of lying or standing on a board, I felt a need to completely give myself to the water. To allow it to hold me like the logs and sticks, the weed and the fish.

We only benefit from something when we give ourselves fully to it. To carefully calculate risk and then trust ourselves enough to take that first step into the unknown builds confidence. It allows new energy to flow into our lives, bringing new perspectives on the world around us. Our minds need fresh energy to push forward and to thrive in life, and we do that by connecting to something new so deeply that we feel it is the right place to be at the right time. Knowing where we should and shouldn't be, in the rise and fall of life, allows us to embrace that moment, broaden our horizons and move with new energy into a better place of mind.

Sensing in the dark

I have found the darkness anything but dark. I have never returned from the sea and felt that I did not know where I was, where I swam or anything like that. In fact the opposite has been true. The darkness has always shone light through my other senses. The lack of light creates extreme focus in other senses and indeed in vision, or so it has been my experience anyway.

When I was six years old, I was diagnosed with colour blindness. One of the strangest effects of this colour blindness occurs when I am in the sea. I struggle when the light is low just before dark. If I am surfing, particularly on a grey winter's evening, the colour of the sea can sometimes match the colour of the sky and the horizon, to the point that I cannot determine if there is an unbroken wave approaching or not. In May 2023, I raised money for the mental health campaign, Surfing Through Darkness, which involved surfing 154 waves from sunset into the night. As the light dwindled, I began to find it almost impossible to see the waves approach. My friend Richard swam out to help me; he floated a little way offshore and when a wave came, he would call it out as a good one and I would catch it.

It is rarely pitch black when I swim. At times, the sea can be extremely bright, with moonlight creating a scene as if in a black-and-white photo. I am drawn to black-and-white images, where there is less colour confusion. Could it be a reason I'm comfortable in the dark seeing the heavy contrast between the dark blackness of the water and the whiteness of the white water after a broken wave? Although there doesn't seem to be any specific supporting research on this, there does seem to be a consensus that people with colour blindness may rely more on contrast to navigate daily life. Personally, I think night swimming may settle the stimuli for me in some way, so I feel more at ease in a black-and-white environment.

Maybe there is more to see on those dark nights than I see, by people who don't have colour blindness. There are no doubt many more shades of darkness and light than I am seeing. About 15 years ago I took a group of people with various degrees of sense impairment out on the water for the day. The feeling of sand between our toes, the feel of neoprene in our hands and on our bodies, the gentle lap of the waves at our feet was a joy. At the water's edge we stopped and let the little waves reach in toward our bare feet. The sense of the cold water was a shock and some danced on their tiptoes. Others stood still. The water drew in around our ankles before flowing back out, as if the sea breathed out toward us to say hello before taking a breath and welcoming us in. It was a magical experience.

Limited vision meant that these swimmers couldn't see the environment they were in, but they did sense it in other ways. There is a similarity between what they experienced in the water and what night swimming is like for me. With night swimming, it is rarely completely pitch black, but there is no doubt that I notice sounds and feel the movement of the water much more than I do when it is daylight. The many distractions in daylight keep me from consciously experiencing the environment I am in with complete attention. Beach-goers, dogs barking ashore, children playing in the shallows and wildlife passing by all hinder my attention to the sea during daylight. At night it's a totally different world.

The light is often so low that vision is impaired when I swim, but instead I tend to notice the smallest of details on, and in, the water. The water holds on to any fragment of light left over from distant streetlights and the moon. The little imperfections in the surface cast shadows which turn the tiniest ripples into a heavily textured expanse of water appearing to move of its own accord across the inky black sea. This can alert me to danger, showing me water that may be moving and water that may be still.

I have not experienced anything else in life that creates this kind of hyper-attentive, aware and focused state, but at the same time it comes from a place of relaxation and calm.

Listen

I am very aware that when I am swimming out among the wild North Atlantic surf at night, I am hearing the sea roar much loader than I normally would. And when the sea is calm and mysteriously black, my ears are working hard. I'm hyper-alert and picking up the tiniest little sound of movement in the water.

Melanie Barratt, a visually impaired swimmer, explains in her blog, "A Blind Swimmer's Vision", how she experiences the water when she swims in the wild: "The experience I have from this type of swimming is very different – it is all about movement, breathing, noise, water in my face, darkness, water rushing over me and my ears." This bears similarities to how I experience night swimming. After the initial stages of trying desperately to see everything in the water, I have found that when I relax into night swimming, it's like my mind opens up to a different, more intricate, view of the world around me.

This awareness begins even before I enter the water. I am hyper-aware and alert as I walk across the beach toward the sea, in darkness. I find myself listening intently for other people who may see me entering the water. I do not want to unnecessarily raise concern in anyone for my safety.

As I wade out into the dark waters, I find my ears notice the sound of the water much more than during daylight. As the sense of sight diminishes, it seems like my sense of hearing improves. The sea is louder, almost overwhelming on stormy nights. Maybe my brain amplifies the sound to warn me that the sea is wild and to be careful. My ears flood with the constant white noise of roaring waves as they rush in from the dark horizon. The wind sometimes roars too, making the whole experience extremely stimulating.

A calming place

A few years ago, I realized that I struggle with over-stimulation with regards to lighting, sound and crowds, which can also be neurodivergent traits. I find lots of noise and chaotic environments uncomfortable. I find it hard to talk to someone if there is background noise, anything from the dishwasher being loaded, to traffic. I can't concentrate on work unless there is silence or, strangely ... rhythmic death metal or hardcore punk! So, for me to be drawn to, and at ease, in the noisy, chaotic environment of water after sundown, might sound counter-intuitive. Night swimming has shone light on the existence of these traits in me that I otherwise hadn't noticed. It wasn't until I started night swimming that I thought I may have some form of undiagnosed neurodivergence.

In March 2024, *The Irish Times* reported on a survey about neurodivergence. The study revealed that one in ten people consider themselves neurodivergent, yet only half of those have a diagnosis. I have discovered that colour blindness is considered neurodiverse, and colour blindness is often present in people with other neurodiverse traits, too.

I have drawn the conclusion that, for me, the lack of light during night swimming subconsciously calms me, despite the constant and often wild, erratic noise of the sea. Once I tune in and listen to what I'm hearing, my ears show me my way through the wild surf as I swim. After several years of night swimming, I now believe this is why I love the extreme wild conditions. Perhaps unexpectedly, I find the calm, dark nights in the water to be much more dangerous. While those nights may seem inviting, in my experience they create a false sense of security. There is no crashing surf, no clash of rip currents against white water and no wind blowing the spray off the waves to rain down on me. On those calm nights, I struggle to see and hear, and so despite the assumption that the water is safer because it is calmer, for me, it is more dangerous, because there is very little for my senses to pick up on to guide me through the dark. And it makes perfect sense. If our sight is hindered by light, we need the water to stimulate our other senses or we become lost in the dark.

Swimming through the fog

There have been night swims where I have sensed extreme danger because of the lack of information for my other senses to gather. In night swimming you will experience varying degrees of light, wind, cold and many other elements. I've usually found that there is enough information for me to be in the water, when combined with my own knowledge of the area and the conditions. But there was one night, 3 December 2023, where I felt extremely vulnerable.

The coast was cloaked in the heaviest sea fog I have ever seen. Sea fog is one of the most dangerous conditions to be in the sea, be it day or night-time. It is extremely disorientating. In daylight it is possible to find my way ashore if the glare from the sun is enough to break through the fog and help me get some sort of bearing, but at night, heavy sea fog is a major issue.

One night I was in the middle of a charity fundraising swim campaign, and I felt that, if I didn't swim, I would be letting supporters down. The whole message of the campaign was to keep "swimming through darkness", to keep going no matter what. I felt that if I didn't swim that night, I would be demonstrating that I wasn't prepared to keep swimming through the darkness no matter the conditions, and it would undermine the message of the campaign. However, I know it's crucial to recognize when conditions become too dangerous and to always prioritize safety. My experience reminds me that no one should ever underestimate the unpredictable risks posed by fog, darkness or changing water conditions.

So, I headed out there onto the beach in the dark and fog. On foggy nights the moisture in the air tends to magnify the sound of the sea. So, if there are any waves at all, the sound of them breaking will make the waves sound much larger and more powerful than they are. The crashing sound of the surf will travel much further, too. I stood on the beach that day, to assess the situation. There were virtually no waves, so I was sure that would still be the case after dark.

My plan was to head along the beach to the west and then swim back using the local current to help. I jogged in the heavy fog about a mile before walking to the water's edge. Being alone in the fog was eerie. I often keep an eye on skylines and lights in the distance when I'm on the beach, just in case someone may be there, but to be completely blind to that was unnerving.

I waded out into the water. It was eerily dark and calm, with the thick layer of fog completely obscuring the moon from sight. I lay nervously in the shallows, conscious of the hard and heavily compacted sand below the surface. There was complete blackness to the north where the lights on the headland, normally visible, were completely obscured from sight. I could not see the shore at all, despite staying close. It was the most isolating experience I have ever had. I began to swim to the east, reaching my hand ahead of me into the black to propel me forward. With each stroke I reached down to make sure my fingers could touch the sand, and with each kick of my feet I reached out my toes to be sure they too could touch the sand. I was slightly panicked by the conditions, but I was super-alert, feeling energized and excited. I completed the swim back to the end of the beach using my GPS watch, so I knew how far I had swum and where I was in relation to my car.

One reason I am so drawn to night swimming is that it continually throws difficult scenarios at me and offers me the chance to improve myself, overcome challenges and make a difference to others. It is very powerful. I knew that it meant a lot to the campaign's supporters that I did this and kept the message strong.

The next morning, after the fog had cleared, I returned to the beach. I found a ragged and torn piece of white fibre glass, complete with navigation light and handrail still attached. I spoke to the beach manager and discovered that a trawler crew had become disorientated in the heavy fog, and their 30-ft boat capsized against the big tide. Four men were thrown into the sea. Thankfully, the men were saved but the boat was destroyed. I have since found numerous parts of it in the water during my night swims.

This is a sign that you always need to stay alert, even when you have everything planned and you have checked all the usual conditions, because sometimes you just don't know what may be in the water, hidden by the tide, by the darkness. And that is also true of life.*

---

* Although this was a successful swim for me, I do not recommend swimming in low or poor visibility. The unpredictability of these conditions is extreme and swimming should not be attempted.

So, should you night swim?

It's important to remember that night swimming requires thorough preparation, knowledge of the conditions, and the ability to assess your own limits. No matter how confident or experienced you are, you are not invincible. Always approach the water with caution and awareness of the risks involved and make your own sensible judgements and assessments of what you are doing.

As you can see, there is a spectrum of what night swimming is. There are different levels of dark, varying conditions, different abilities and desires as to what night swimming may be to each person. To stand safely in the shallows with your eyes closed may be enough for you to experience night swimming. As you gain experience and a deeper understanding of your local waters, you may find yourself drawn to swim in different environments or conditions. But no matter where you are on this spectrum, night swimming can bring great light to our lives, through heightened awareness, deeper experience, hyper-focus and undistracted immersion in the elements.

CHAPTER 3

HOW THE SEA BECAME THE MOON

I was floating on my back under a sea of stars on a cold autumn night. Clad head-to-toe in black neoprene, I blended with the gentle midnight swell beyond the basalt rocks on the shore. The village was silent as everyone hid inside, away from the pandemic. There was no wind, just the rhythmic wash of the little swell collapsing on the edge of the beach. The only cloud in sight was that from the warmth of my breath floating in the cold air. I drifted in the shallows immersed in contentment and peace, as each swell lifted and gently set me back for the next. In a time of darkness and uncertainty, I realized, swimming at night had lit up the darkness.

The moon and our mood

For centuries it has been believed that the moon affects mental health. Many other parts of life have also been attributed to, or connected to, the cycles of the moon such as the menstrual cycle, intensity of illness, and even violence and crime. The word lunacy derives from the Latin *lunaticus,* meaning "moonstruck", which came from behaviours believed to be associated with the moon. Although science does not seem to agree with this line of thinking, for these beliefs to have lasted through time, truth must lie in them, to some degree. In our modern lives, we can become disconnected from the moon. I have found night swimming has helped me reconnect.

How to find your moon

Sometimes the lives we live are not necessarily the lives we planned for ourselves. For a variety of reasons, we let go of the passions that kept us afloat as we grew into the world as children. The current of life lifted us and took us with it, meandering its way through all sorts of good times and not such good times. Decisions we made led to experiences so powerful that we forgot some of the things that made us happy and who we are. In this fast-paced world there are many of us struggling to keep our heads above water. Life can be overwhelming and the thought that stopping treading water to do something that might help us live a more fulfilled life seems counterproductive. But we need to. We need to find what gives us purpose and presence of mind.

When the moon rises into the night sky, it brings light to a seemingly endless darkness. Its size and power achieve the impossible task of brightening the night, just enough that we can find our way. I believe we all need to find our own moon to allow us to persevere through the hours of darkness that from time to time fall within our own personal lives. A hobby, a friend, a place . . . whatever it is, we all need our own unique light that stops us losing hope in the darkest times of our life. Allowing its light to seep into the shadows, our moon can gradually defeat the dark.

To find your moon, you might first need to reflect on various parts of your life. Maybe it relates to loss, love or decisions you made at some point that has led to where you are today. I think as we grow through life we often look back at points in our lives and wonder how things might have been had we done things differently. In hindsight we can often see the path we took more clearly than we do in the moment, and that may lead to us wondering if we went the best way. But we need to remember that the best way forward starts here, today. From here we can take that experience and move forward. We can't go back.

The sea is my moon

My dad was a fisherman and so, as a child, if I wasn't playing on the beach or in the shallows, I was in a boat or standing on a pier as he fished. I have known the sea longer than I've known most people in my life. I am more comfortable and at ease in the sea than I am in any other situation in life.

I think it was April 2000 when I first realized that I find the sea as some kind of saviour for me. I had just returned home from the funeral of a local man. It was a grey, cold afternoon, and I came home feeling distraught and angry about everything. I can't even remember getting changed but I do remember running in my wetsuit with my surfboard so fast over the sand dunes and onto the beach that my feet could barely keep up. I ran across the blowy white sand and continued until I was deep enough in water to dive onto my board and paddle out through the white-water waves. It felt like a natural reaction to what I was experiencing. The sea kept me occupied until dark.

Since then, I can think of many other occasions when I have gone to the sea in difficult times. I don't sit out there and contemplate anything. I don't particularly surf well in that moment and I don't even care about the conditions. The sea just seems to be where I go and what I do. I just go out there and my thoughts drift between the thing bothering me and then back to the water, watching the sea rise and fall, reading the water and catching waves.

Sometimes I go without my board and bodysurf my way through the thoughts, swimming into the path of unbroken waves, matching their speed and energy and gliding with them like a dolphin through the water. I assume that the presence of mind and body, combined with instinct, distracts my mind from the real world while I'm engaged in the water. The physical touch of the water, its motion and energy keeping me focused until clarity of mind returns. One time recently I didn't even go in the sea – I just walked for miles and miles in the shallows of the river estuary near where I live. The ripples in the hard sand below the water mesmerized me as I walked barefoot.

Like the moon creates a focal point in the dark night sky, the sea commands my attention in the darkest moments of life. It provides a place where I become at one with my surroundings, my mind fixated on its patterns and movements. Like a moth to the flame, I rush to the light until I can again find my own way through the dark I'm experiencing.

I began to realize that in all the decisions I make in my life, I need to protect my ability to surf and swim. I need to be able to keep the sea at the centre of my life. It has been there since I was a little kid and to let myself drift away from it would be disastrous to my wellbeing. So, as life has gone on, I've made as many decisions hinge around it as I can. I know lots of people who have moved inland to get better jobs, and a better standard of living in some ways, but for me, it makes more sense that I stay by the coast. I do many things to make sure I can maintain my connection to the sea, and in doing so, it is there through the good times and the bad. My life happens next to, in and on the sea. And although I recognize that the water is not a substitute for consulting mental health professionals and experts, nor may my experience be the same as everyone else's, it is without doubt that the sea is at the heart of my wellbeing. The sea is my moon.

Understanding your darkness

The darkness I refer to in night swimming is very obviously the lack of light at night, but the metaphors that have evolved from my discovery of night swimming relate to many other parts of life. Sometimes we can be so deep in a dark phase of life that we are unaware of it. Unfortunately, it may have become so normal to us that we know nothing else. It could be relationship issues, financial struggles, health concerns or simply confusion as to where we are in life at a particular moment. I think there are many more people in this world who feel lost and hopeless at times than we maybe realize. You must remember that no matter what you face, you are not alone, and others are also struggling to find light in their lives.

Before finding your moon, the thing that may help bring light to your life, you need to be able to identify what it is you are facing. We need to embrace the darkness we face before we can truly understand the reason we are in that place, at that time in our life. Once we identify that, we can look deeper into ourselves for the light that may help guide us from it.

Kendra Cherry wrote about the process of problem-solving: "Before problem-solving can occur, it is important to first understand the exact nature of the problem itself. If your understanding of the issue is faulty, your attempts to resolve it will also be incorrect or flawed."

Take a moment to think about that now. Over time you may begin to see what the root cause is. To deal with it, it may be important to be present with it, and ultimately accept it as the root cause of your struggles. But this may be easier said than done. There are many times in life when we find it easier or think it is better for us not to face the thing that we know deep down is causing us to feel low. But, accepting it is a major stage in dealing with it.

You might find it difficult, and it may take several attempts over a period of time to achieve acceptance. If it truly is something that matters to you, then it is important to not give up, and to keep returning until you can be at peace. Accepting it allows you to open the door and let new light into that area of your life to replace the darkness. The sea has been my refuge, providing me with comfort and clarity, but I know that for many, their "moon" may come in different forms. Finding what soothes and supports you during tough times is a deeply personal journey, and it may be helpful to explore multiple avenues that may help.

The darkness holds opportunity

There is a hidden value to darkness. Periods of darkness can lead us into deep reflection and analysis of our life and experiences. I feel that the hardest times I have faced in life have made me who I am. Facing bereavement, loss, betrayal and many other challenges in life have taught me vital lessons that I now carry with me into every other walk of life. Those lessons protect me in the present and the future. So, from the darkest times comes experience and knowledge that we can use to make our lives better. But if we don't face those tough times and use reflection to draw out the lessons, then we don't move forward, we don't grow from the darkness into the light, and instead we stay lost in the shadows. It is important to remember the value of self-reflection, but keeping an open mind to and seeking external support is just as important to overcoming tough times.

I count myself very fortunate to have had the sea so prominent in my life and an important part of my wellbeing. I know some people lose who they are as they move and adapt to life's challenges. Before they even realize it, they are somewhere they didn't plan to be, doing something that was never their dream and maybe surrounded by people they didn't think would be in their life. It can be very difficult to look past all that and find any constant in life, but with some deliberate action it is possible to find your way again.

A spark of light

The first little spark of light in dark times may go unnoticed. And it doesn't have to be swimming! It could be a new person in your life, a return to playing sport with old friends or something creative you did as a child or teenager, but put aside until recently. Some examples from my friends' lives are: going to the gym, music, playing instruments and helping others. Helping others can be a light in your life and in theirs, providing warmth, connection and positivity through the dark times.

These are all things that may not seem out of the ordinary, but may, in fact, be the light returning to your life. We are often so caught up in feeling low that a little thing that breaks through the darkness goes unnoticed. We need to take action to embrace this little spark and allow it to grow. We need to recognize it, and nurture it, until it grows into a positive light in our lives that helps us to grow out of the darkness we face. Alex Lickerman MD wrote an article in psychologytoday.com about trying new things: "Growth seems to require we take new action first, whether it's adopting a new attitude or a new way of thinking, or literally taking new action. Thrusting yourself into new situations and leaving yourself there alone, so to speak, often forces beneficial change."

I believe that when we take action to embrace something new, or restart something we put aside many years ago, that our world changes in ways beyond the activity. The sea has opened my life to opportunity, new people and amazing experiences. It has kept me focused and given me release, good energy flow, hope, opportunity and happiness, no matter what was going on in life. It gives me a natural buzz and lift in my energy that lasts for hours, days and even weeks, in some cases. Life is for living: it should be exhilarating, exciting and full of good times. But we need to take action to allow that into our life. We need to choose the things that set us alight and move us out of the darkness.

Keeping a daily log

Ever since I was a kid, I have written almost every day. I lived in the country and had no friends nearby, so I spent my evenings writing music, playing my guitar and noting down the events of the day. I think daily writing was probably a method I used to understand life. Writing things out allowed me to think clearly, identify patterns and make sense of life.

When I was young, I was probably unaware that the connection to the sea combined with writing was helping me find my way. I still write and go in the sea every day; that has not changed. To help you find your moon, you too could start writing every day. It doesn't matter what you write about, or how much. You might write a few notes, or pages and pages of stuff you need to get out of your mind. This is purely for you to read. No one is going be looking over your shoulder and marking your spelling and grammar. It doesn't even need to make sense. Once you have done this for a week or two, get all the notes together and ask yourself these questions:

- Are there things that you are doing every day that you enjoy and bring fun or excitement to your life?

- What are the things that are happening that are bothering you?

- Are there reoccurring fears and anxieties that seem to be coming up in your daily notes?

The beauty of writing a daily log is that you can attempt to find your way through the darkness you are facing by asking yourself questions about the things you have written down. You start to see your daily life and habits and may begin to recognize the areas of life that make you feel good and the ones that don't.

A moment of calm

When I was a teenager, I wanted to take my surfing to a new level. I had competed in Ireland, but I wanted to push to the next level of competing on the British Pro Surfing Tour. I felt I was ready for it, and I moved to England to do it. There, I was confronted with lots of good surfers, many more than I had ever seen in one place. It was a shock. I froze up in competition and didn't do very well. It led me into a dark time where I felt like I wasn't able to snap out of this negative mindset and allow myself to surf to the best of my abilities. I decided I needed to take action. I went to the library at the University of Plymouth to find sports psychology books. I listened to sports psychology cassette tapes when I slept at night. I visited a renowned hypnotherapist in Belfast who taught me a beneficial technique that I wish to share with you.

The technique was to close my eyes and think only about the darkness I could see. Then he made me visualize a tiny little prick of white light in the darkness and I had to shift my focus to that. I had to keep my attention on this little glimmer of hope in the darkness, this little moon in the vast expanse of darkness all around me. Once I was completely focused on it, the hypnotist told me to place my middle finger on the centre of my forehead. I had to focus on it and let the light move to the point where my finger rested. It made me feel like everything came back to the centre. I've found this technique useful when life is busy and chaotic, and I use it to this day.

Embrace your moon

My moon, the sea, has guided me daily through many of life's challenges. It balances my days and my nights. It brings a constant source of power to my world. I believe we all need this in our lives, and it doesn't need to be night swimming or the sea that provides light for you. Although it can be, and we will look at that in the next chapter. Your moon can be anything that brings a positive light to your life. Just like the moon pulls the tides, your moon will draw you through the darkest times of your life. Give time and attention to finding it, and once you do, allow its embrace to pull you out of the shadows and back into the light where you belong!

CHAPTER 4

THE LANGUAGE OF
THE SEA

The sea has no words to speak but it can be understood it many other ways. Its mysterious communication style leaves clues and hints to its behaviour for water users to read. Piecing these little notes together leads a swimmer into an exclusive world. This world is reserved for lovers of the ocean. As a lover of the ocean, you feel its pulse, its draw of breath before its raging outburst and thrashing of the coast. You hear it lying gently by the shoreline, whispering its presence. You see it reach out, touching and caressing the coast. You know this wild beast and gentle old soul so intimately that you can, to some degree, predict its next move. Knowing when to swim and when to sit it out and enjoy a coffee on the beach instead is a skill developed over time.

The writer CS Lewis and his family used to holiday near where I live in Castlerock. His mother apparently once commented that she disliked it here because the sea is too noisy. The sea can be raging or flat calm and still a persistent white noise fills the village sea air. I've been all over the world and not experienced such a vocal sea as that touching the shore in Castlerock. It can be heard clearly through closed doors and windows. Why is the sea so noisy here? What is it trying to say?

Immersion

Not all language is verbal. The sea signals and leaves messages informing you of how and why it behaves as it does. Its body language often telegraphs its intentions. When you are in another country you can pick up the local lingo, often understanding when someone is asking what you would like to eat. After a few days you can probably say hello and thank you. In those few days you learned how to survive by picking up the basics of the language. However, as soon as you go home you probably forget it all because you don't need it. Imagine how much you would learn if you stayed "deep in the sea" of this foreign vocabulary. You would begin to understand the nuances of the language, the colloquialisms and the local cultural influences and accents that all develop from the same basic words on paper.

The sea may speak the same language all over the planet, but it too has a different accent in each place. Its tongue contorts and assumes the form of the local rises and falls of the seabed (bathymetry) differently in every cove and bay on earth.

An article on Robertsonslanguage.com, titled, "Why immersive learning is the best way to learn a new language", explains that: "The reason why immersion learning really works is that it puts your language learning in context. That's why people who move to a new country appear to pick up a language at breakneck speed – they have to live, interact and carry out day-to-day tasks as normal . . . Except they are doing it in their new language."

This is true of the sea. Fishing folk, surfers and swimmers know the waters intimately through complete immersion in its world. However, they pick up the language of the sea in different ways because of the context of how and where they place themselves within it. The fisherman reads signs from the ocean about water depth, currents and surface movement so that he can predict where to fish. The surfer knows what lies on the seabed that shapes the approaching swell into the wave she wants to catch. The swimmer knows when and where the tide is at its weakest because he wants to swim without its resistance.

Tides

Like a silk glove pulled slowly over an old working hand, the tide slides over every crease, scar and knuckle of rock along the shore. Scars of daily life are concealed by this pulse of the sea.

The tide is the earth's pulse. Its power reaches far beyond the oceans. It swells up estuaries and rivers, bringing a new cycle of the planet's energy, several times a day. By observing a tide pattern, noticing when it retreats and when it reaches up closer to us, we can become more aware of the earth's positive energy.

It is worth noting that the tide doesn't simply move out and in along straight lines. The tide moves in all directions as it fills into, and drains out of, the coastline. This results in water constantly flowing in different directions as opposed to how it may appear on the surface, where it simply moves in and out on the beach. Tides can reach far inland as it floods up into estuaries, rivers and loughs/ lochs and can reach lakes, such as Pitt Lake in British Columbia. So, even if you plan to swim inland, check if the water is tidal!

The tide usually slackens in speed around high and low tide times. The fastest movement in tide tends to happen in the third hour of tide, in most locations. So, the bigger the tidal range (the difference between the measurements of low tide and high tide), the quicker the water will be moving. All tides in the UK are based upon a level at Newlyn Observatory in Cornwall. Other countries use their own levels and terminology and those can be found online for Canada, USA, Australia, etc. In the UK, the tide times for all other tidal places, can be predicted from the tide level at Newlyn. You can get information on your local area, or a point close by in newspapers, fishing forecasts, pocket tide charts, a tide atlas or online. If I ever look up tides online, I use www.tidetimes.org.uk.

Where I swim, the tide drains to the east and fills to the west/northwest. The tide will be higher in towns to the east of me before it peaks where I swim. I can feel the water change when the tide backs off the high – the energy slackens as the waves tend to decrease in both size and frequency.

Observing your swim spot around the predicted highs and lows is a good start. Spend time observing how and when the tide fills and drains. This will teach you what is the most likely movement in your area when you swim. And that is all we are trying to do here; we can't predict everything, and it would be boring to do so. If you can establish the most likely eventuality for water moving in relation to the tide then that is a great start to knowing and trusting the water to behave as you would expect. While developing an intimate understanding of local conditions is invaluable, it is important to always prioritize safety and never underestimate the power of the sea. No matter how well you understand water, there is always risk involved.

I live on the shores of the North Channel, between Ireland and Scotland. The coast here is exposed to one of the strongest tidal flows in the world, and it is a famous stretch of water because of this tide. It is challenging to navigate with a boat, but it is also one of the most dangerous crossings for swimmers and so attracts the most hardcore athletes on the planet, all hoping to be able to overcome the deadly currents and swim across. In areas with strong tidal flows, such as the North Channel, swimming without proper safety equipment or expert guidance is not advisable. It is important to assess the conditions and your own ability thoroughly before entering water. Not all water is suitable for all abilities!

The tide here is the clash of the Irish Sea and the Atlantic being pushed and pulled through a narrow channel, forming raging currents and whirlpools just offshore. The water tends to flow to the east/southeast when the tide is dropping, and to the northwest when it is rising. Standing on the coast it appears like the tide is going in and out, but it is not that simple. I once challenged myself to paddle a board between the Giant's Causeway and Islay, against this tide. I gleaned local knowledge from old salty sea-dogs and from a tidal atlas. I worked out the direction of the tidal flow for every hour of the cycle, to allow me to choose the right time to enter the water. I plotted my way across the channel before the tide turned, which meant calculating my approximate speed, if everything went to plan. I also worked out the speed of the tidal flow at various stages of the crossing, as it flowed with me and then against me.

But I was still met with several factors that I did not anticipate, including the tide around Jura clashing with the North Channel, driving me west off my proposed landing spot. It took over nine hours, against a tide so strong that if I stopped paddling at all, the current would take me backward.

When to enter the water

The right time for you to enter the water will depend on what you are doing, where you are swimming and your ability. I would suggest looking at your tidal information and establishing the slackest time periods in the tide movement. That will usually be close to high or low tide and when there is less flow.

But be aware that the water is never completely still. Just because it may say something on paper doesn't mean it is fact; tide tables are simply predictions based on the past. Tidal predictions may not allow for local weather and environmental factors that may increase or decrease the figures given on the tidal table. Always use a combination of observation, experience and information when making any decisions about the water and never rely solely on one source.

Tidal ranges

High tide is the term used to describe the position of the tide when it is at its highest level. This level changes with every high tide. Conversely, the term low tide is the opposite and is used to describe the position of the tide when it is at its lowest point. The space between high and low is the tidal range.

In some locations, tides don't play a huge role and that may be a safer place to swim than the exposed shores of the Atlantic. Some parts of the world have much smaller tides: for example, the smallest tidal range is in the Gulf of Mexico, with less than a metre (a yard) of movement.

The world's largest tidal range is in the Bay of Fundy, Canada, with a staggering 11-metre (36-foot) range. With the fastest tides in the world peaking at around 40 kmph (25 mph) and the average swimmer moving at around 1.6 kmph (1 mph), you will be no match for the sea.

Spending time listening, watching and learning from the movement of the ocean for any clues or hints about the tide is crucial to being an open-water swimmer.

The term "spring tide" is used to describe a tide just after a new or full moon, when there is the greatest difference between high and low tide. The term "neap tide" is used to describe the smallest difference between high and low tide. A neap tide can be a safer time to swim where tides may have a less significant influence on the water.

Tide charts and atlases

It used to be that we all carried a little paper booklet, a tide chart, around with us, containing predictions of the tide in the local area, and these are still available. However, this information is now available online on sites such as Tidetimes.org.

The tide chart shows the height of the tide in metres or feet, at different times of the day.

If you swim on the coast, you may be able to source a copy of a tidal atlas showing tide flows, direction of flow, counter flows and speeds. From that you will be able to work out the various stages of tide flow for your area, for the various times of day and night.

A tidal atlas is an amazing window into a world you may already know, but with this extra detail it brings you even closer to it. The one I use is called *Admiralty Tidal Stream Atlas*, and it shows movement all around the UK and Ireland including into some loughs/lochs and estuaries. If you live next to a river that floods from the sea, you can find flow information from the National River Flow Archive in the UK or USGS in the USA.

How to use a tide chart

Start by referencing the tide chart, and observe the position of the tide at the predicted time of high water at your chosen swim spot. If you visit the swim spot at various times of the year, when the tide chart is giving the same or a similar figure in height, you will most likely notice that the water is not always in the same place. This is because the tide level is affected by many other elements, so although tides are predictable, it is not possible to solely rely on this information to plan being in or around the water. For example, high winds, big surf or localized flooding could magnify the energy in the water making the water appear higher up the beach than it may do if the weather was calm.

When you are observing the high tide, take note of anything you think may be significant if you were swimming. Are there any obvious signs of water movement? It may be that there is a consistent local

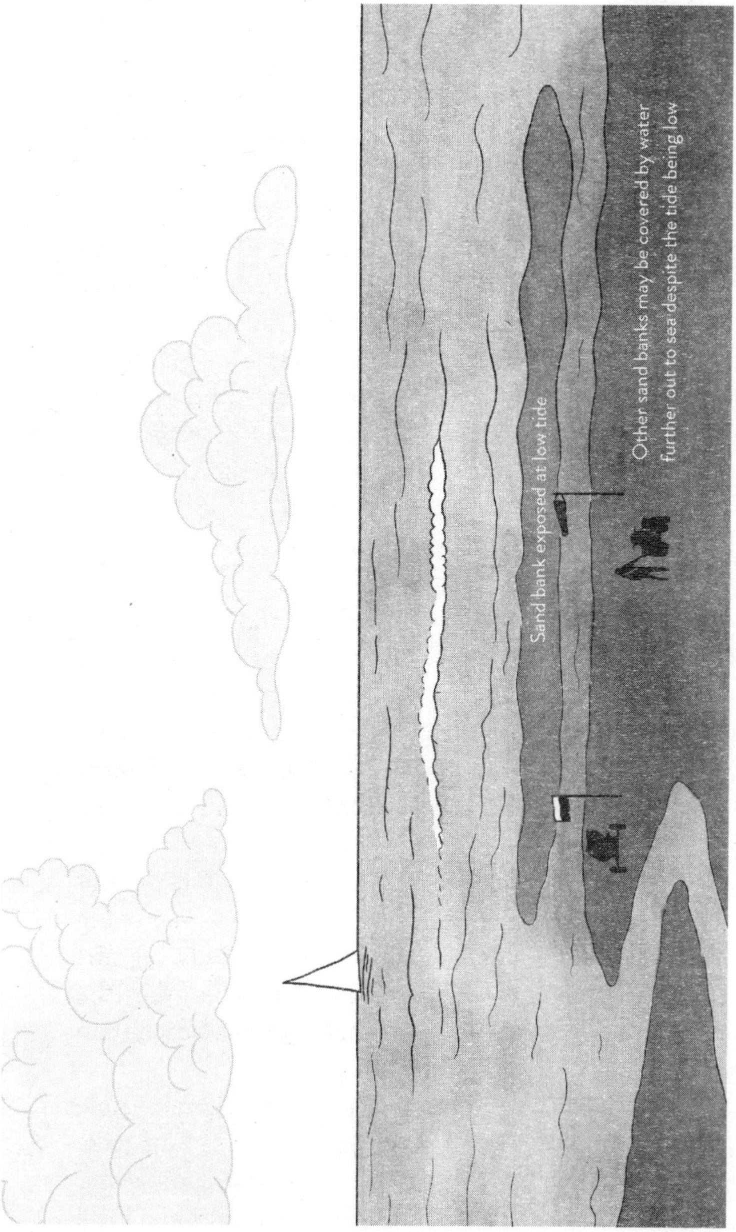

Sand bank exposed at low tide

Other sand banks may be covered by water further out to sea despite the tide being low

Figure 1: Sand bar

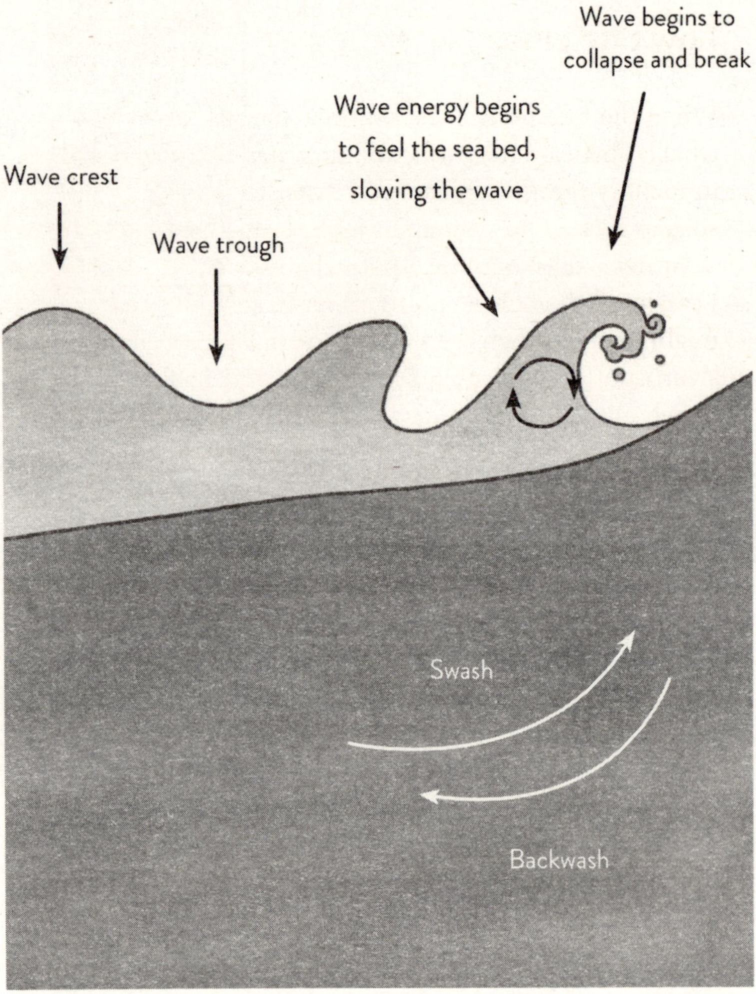

Figure 2: Characteristics of waves

flow of water, a rip current, or underwater contours in the seabed that may not be visible unless the tide is out. Observing the tide is a good start to reading the water and you can begin before you even step into the sea.

Low tide clues

When the tide pulls back you may have a clear view of what lay beneath the surface of the water. You may be able to identify things that caused or assisted the water flow such as rock groins, channels in the seabed, etc.

At my local swimming spot, when the sea pulls back, I can look at the distribution of sand to think about what might happen when the tide is back in later. Maybe your swim spot is rockier or deeper than mine. If you look closely at Figure 1, behind where the lifeguards are set up, you will notice a shallow area of water running parallel to the sea. If you follow it in either direction, you will notice that it enters the sea at either end of a raised section of sand. That raised section of sand is a sand bar. That sand bar is there all year round, although it does change shape and size, depending on the weather.

Swell

"Swell" is the term used to describe the energy that has transferred from the wind into the ocean. The pressure from the wind forces the water away from the centre of a storm, and as the energy travels through the water it begins to form undulations on the surface of the water. Imagine dropping a pebble into a puddle – the rings of water that travel toward the edge of the puddle are

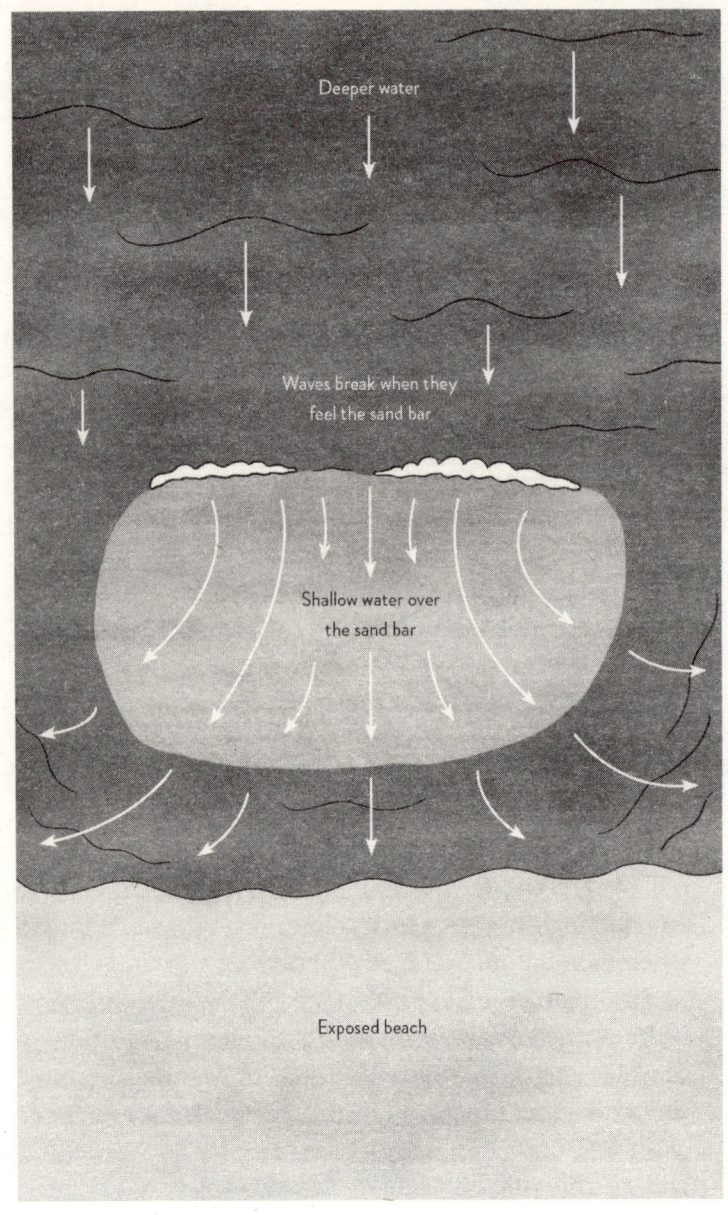

Deeper water

Waves break when they
feel the sand bar

Shallow water over
the sand bar

Exposed beach

Figure 3: Low tide clues

effectively lines of swell, on a smaller scale. Sea swells can range from a mild ripple to around 20 metres (65 feet) in height! When swells from far out at sea arrive at the coast, they usually show some of their energy above the surface, while the rest of the energy is below the surface, out of sight.

As the waves approach the coast, the underwater wave energy feels the shallow water, which in this case, is above a sand bank.

The swell is slowed by the shallow water until it slows so much that it collapses into a wave.

This white-water wave rushes over the sand bank, but all this energy must go somewhere. It doesn't continue to rush inland forever – it eventually dissipates as the wave's energy diminishes. But the water must return to the sea. The water from the wave falls off the back of the sand bank and the water starts to find its way back out to sea, flowing in the channel to the left and the right.

Imagine when this energy and movement is all underwater and there is virtually no visible sign of the water moving back out to sea. It simply appears like waves are breaking and washing ashore. But, under the water, the water from the wave is working its way back out to sea through channels in the sand. If there are consistent waves, then this process continues and that is when momentum builds and a current forms.

The channels on my beach are relatively shallow, and if the waves are big or the tide extremely high, the flow of water isn't as definitive as it may appear. In that case, the water surges back and forth, and the incoming waves clash and thrash around, making it very turbulent. You will see this wherever you are, on big surf days or where

Figure 4: High tide clues at my swim spot

Sand bank covered at high tide

waves wash against a man-made structure and then turn back out to sea.

Now look at Figure 4 with the tide high. Notice the lifeguards are still set up in the same place, but the tide is now high. The sandbank is submerged, and so too are the channels in the seabed. The wind is from the east and the tidal flow at this stage is predominantly in the same direction, because it is rising. It is a fairly safe bet that the water will be flowing through those underwater channels to the left, at least until the tide slackens off and then turns. Once it turns it might become a bit more chaotic and choppier for a while, depending on factors such as if the waves get bigger or if the wind stays the same direction. The scene will change constantly throughout every minute of the day and night, with the change in weather and tide.

Seasonal changes

You will notice changes to the sea through the seasons. The sandbanks at my swim spot change constantly with storms, with more powerful tides and wind. So, although the currents in this area are predominantly in the same place, they do shift around and so it is always worth remembering that if you looked at a location in advance, it may have changed to some degree by the time you go swimming.

Nothing is constant with the sea; everything is fluid and constantly adapting to the elements forced upon it. You too must be fluid in your approach to swimming.

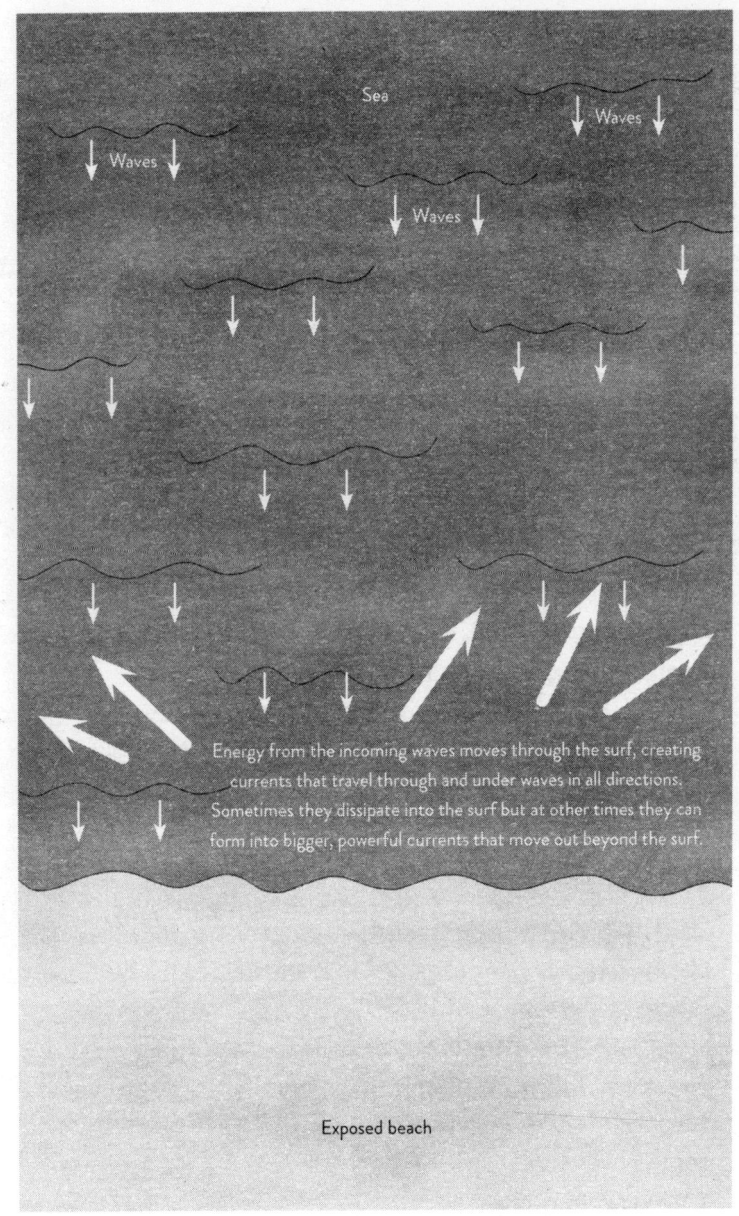

Figure 5: Rip currents

Winter tides

Where I swim, the winter weather can have a dramatic effect on the tides. A big storm can drive the high tide water into the sand dunes, cutting cliffs into the face of the dunes. The lower tides in winter can bring extremely cold water to the shore from two nearby rivers that flow into the sea.

Summer tides

Summer is often the calmest time to start sea swimming. In summer there is usually less wave action, as the water doesn't have the same energy. However, we still need to observe the sea, and be cautious. There is a phenomenon known as the "inverted barometer effect": the high pressure from a summer weather pattern on a sunny day can put so much pressure on the surface of the water that it forces a lower-than-normal tide. Where I swim, that equates to being able to walk past the sea cliffs and into caves, which often leads to unsuspecting tourists getting caught by the tide! This tide will also bring warmer water from the nearby rivers.

Currents

A current is a continuous flow of water in a general direction, and you will find that they are all unique, even ones that appear in the same area. Power, speed, shape, depth and temperature are all factors that influence a current of water, so it will never be the same from one moment to the next. Over time, you can build up

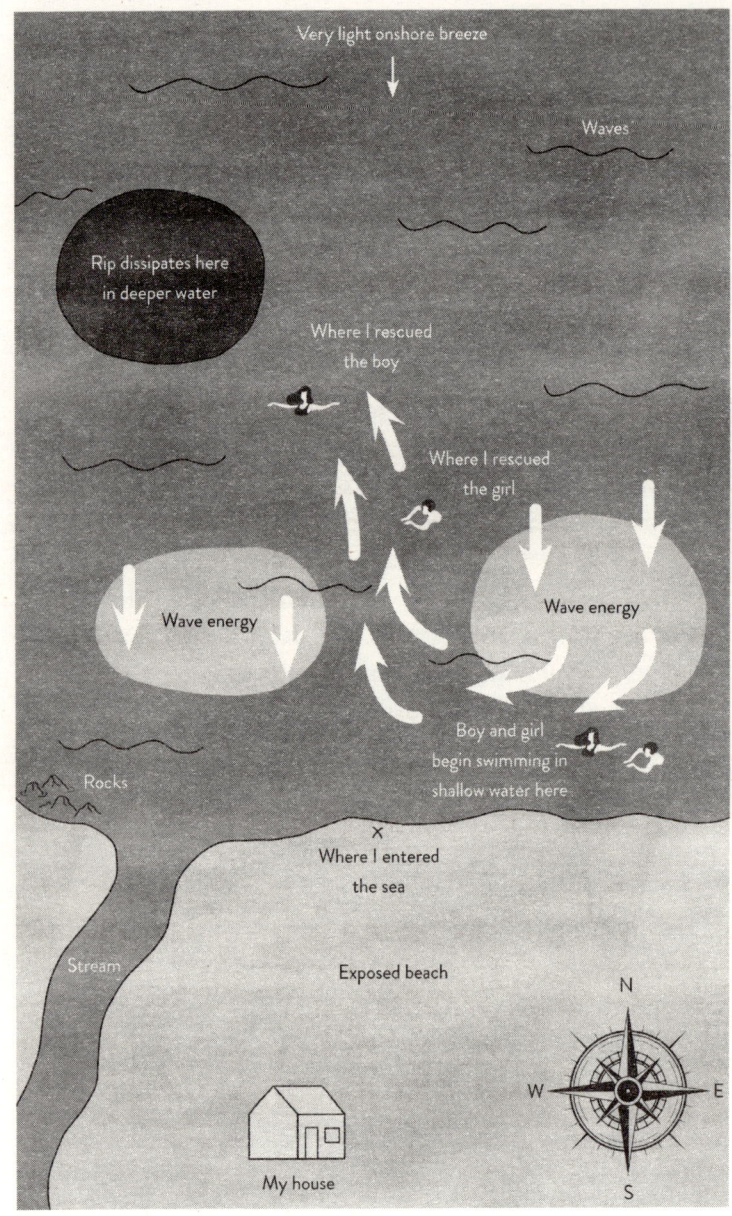

Figure 6: Rip current rescues

knowledge of local currents, through identifying various geographical characteristics and weather and how they affect the water you plan to swim in. But we should still always remain careful.

Rip currents

One term that you may have heard used to describe currents that are often deemed responsible for swimmers getting into difficulty is "rip" current. A rip current is defined as an "intermittent strong surface current flowing seaward from the shore". I would only partially agree with this definition. Rip currents can actually flow in almost all directions, and are not simply surface currents. They can run deep into the water and move at serious speed, but they can also be gentle flowing, so much so that they are almost unrecognizable. They often begin by traversing the shoreline through the surf zone and sandbanks before eventually turning seaward. Rip currents can form unpredictably and may appear deceptively calm. Even experienced swimmers need to be constantly alert to these currents, as they can quickly turn dangerous. If you are unsure, always err on the side of caution and consult a local lifeguard or expert.

It must be noted that although there are many textbook examples of rip currents, there is no one definitive example of what a rip current is. Much of the information is out there to prevent tragedies, but with the very nature of rip currents being so unique, the information is often misleading and difficult to use.

To give some perspective on how frequently rip currents form, as a surfer and a swimmer I am in a rip current almost every time I am in the sea! They are a regular feature of the sea, and just as you expect fish to swim in the sea, you should expect that rip currents exist in it, too. Experienced surfers use rip currents to get from one area of the beach to another, saving their energy by allowing the current to move them, instead of paddling. Surfers are so in tune with the sea that they can put themselves in what may appear to be a dangerous situation to onlookers, but in fact, they are experts in current dynamics.

Rip currents tend to form temporarily and then disappear again, to varying degrees. Sometimes they dissipate into the surf and sometimes they gather power and flow out through channels in the seabed and the surf. They are not always visible as raging torrents of water and that is why they tend to cause issues for the unaware water user. They can be quickly forming, fast moving bodies of water that at times give very little indication that they are even present.

With experience you will be able to identify when some rip currents are about to form and therefore take action to avoid them. Time spent studying waves breaking, and watching where the broken white water moves to as it begins to find its way back to sea, is a good starting point to help you identify rip currents. There is no substitute for spending time observing your local area in various conditions to identify them.

A common myth is that rip currents only happen where the waves don't break. It is true that rip currents do form where waves don't break, but it is not the only place they form!

In fact, the most violent waves are often happening because the rip currents are pushing into the incoming waves, allowing them to stand taller and break harder.

At the big wave surf spot of Nazaré, Portugal, the energy from the waves moves to the south then forms into a giant rip current along the cliff edge and pushes into the incoming massive peaks of swells, forcing them to stand tall and break with immense power. Please don't swim at Nazaré. This is an obvious example of a rip current in action helping to magnify the wave energy. Every location is different so do not assume anything!

Places you will often see rip currents are near:

- **Manmade structures.** Structures built in the natural environment, such as a pier or sea wall, often disrupt flow. Look along the edges of a pier and you will sometimes see deep gouges cut in the seabed, from a regular rip current.

- **Rocks on the beach.** When the tide is out, look around the exposed rocks and you might notice deeper water close to the rocks. Rip currents may be the reason for the sand being eroded here.

- **Beaches.** Anywhere with waves has currents and anywhere without waves also has currents, so that means many beaches. Do not make the mistake of assuming that because there is no surf, there are no currents. I see people caught out by this all the time in summer, particularly cold-water sea swimmers and dippers who are not locals to the area.

- **Streams or rivers entering the sea.** Streams and rivers bring surface run-off, waterfalls and storm-water to the sea. This clash of fresh water with saltwater tends to make the water unstable between the shoreline and the waves. The water can be turbulent even though it may not appear so on the surface. Rip currents often form in that vicinity.

I see currents and rip currents several times a day, and I often see swimmers unknowingly floating in them, but the energy dissipates before there is any real cause for concern. Rip currents happen in all sorts of conditions and that is why they are difficult to identify and educate people about. For that reason, understanding rip currents takes time and experience. I encourage you to focus your efforts on becoming highly in tune to one area for sea swimming rather than several, so you get to understand that area of the sea more safely.

Just as rip currents can vary in size, power and depth, they can also vary in duration. A rip current next to a pier may run almost constantly, if there is enough surf or wind feeding the water along the coast toward it. Some rip currents in the surf may appear for less than a minute. The variations and possibilities are infinite and therefore, as swimmers, we must approach rip currents with a dynamic outlook.

THE DANGER OF RIP CURRENTS

On 18 September 2019, the rip currents around the sandbank in front of my house almost took two lives. A 13-year-old girl and her early-20s big brother were swimming in the surf to the right-hand side of the sandbank. I noticed that they were being pulled to the west, probably through the channel behind the sandbank. As I watched, I grabbed my wetsuit because I was fairly certain what was going to happen next. I see this current every day of the week, so I knew it was almost certain that they would be pulled out to sea in the rip current which was forming.

The pair were about halfway out when they appeared to be getting pulled into the rip. This rip was not the textbook type, flowing straight out to sea – it was about 45 degrees to the beach.

I didn't take my eyes off the water, even for a second. I grabbed a surfboard on the way out and ran down the beach. A small crowd had gathered at this stage, watching, as the pair were sucked quickly out through the breaking waves.

I raced out through the surf to find the brother bravely holding his sister above the water. I pulled the girl onto my board. I deemed it unsafe to do a double rescue and promised him I would return. I caught the next wave back into the shore, where I dropped the girl into the arms of someone who was watching. The brother was now swimming against the rip, which was moving faster than he could swim. The waves were constantly breaking over him, obscuring him from my sight as I headed back out there. He had been moved even further to the northwest by the time I reached him, but I got there on my board, and brought him back to shore.

So, although it was a sunny day, with plenty of people on the beach, the rip current made it unsafe to swim. Knowledge of the unique characteristics at your local beach and the bathymetry can be a massive advantage to any water user.

Staying safe

If you plan to swim in the sea, I highly recommend swimming in depths where you can feel the bottom. You should also be able to clearly identify your position with reference points on land. I regularly see people who are out of their depth and struggling to get back into their depth because a current moved them ever so slightly beyond where they began, as they floated or swam. The illusion of "calm" water can give a false sense of security. Boogie boarders, paddleboarders and surfers also need to be aware of rip currents.

Knowing how to escape a rip current begins with knowing how to recognize that one may form. These points may help you understand the factors influencing the water:

1. Identify what factors may cause water to move: for example, wind, tide, surf, streams, heavy rain or snow melt run-off. If any of those are present then there is a high probability that, at some point, a current will form.

2. Observe the water and take note if any of the factors above are making the water move. Remember that not all currents will break the surface and so you need to consider that currents may not be visible, and think where they might be.

3. Determine where is safe: Avoid areas where dangerous currents might form. Always assume that conditions can change unexpectedly and know when swimming is unsafe. Ask local experts for their help

4. If you plan to swim, identify exit points in the eventuality that you are moved by a current and need to get ashore somewhere else. Ideally, you should have places chosen at all four corners of the compass, but some locations may not provide for that. For example, swimmers in a lake probably have more options than those at an exposed beach.

THE DANGER OF WIND CURRENTS

In summer 2023, at Castlerock, two young boys were on low-quality boogie boards, drifting in a strong current created by wind. There were no waves that day, just flat, calm water, but the strong wind formed a current flowing to the northwest. I was walking my dog at another beach when a neighbour rang to tell me, so I raced home and went out to them on a board. They had made the mistake of kicking their feet against the wind and current for half an hour, and so were extremely exhausted and freezing cold. If they had thought about going ashore elsewhere, they wouldn't have had an issue, but they didn't. I brought them in about 300 metres (330 yards) from where they began.

HOW TO ESCAPE A RIP CURRENT

Many Black Belt martial artists will never be in a street fight. That is because they understand the danger and unpredictability of a fight in that environment and are expert at recognizing the signs and events that may lead to a street fight, so avoid it! That is the level all swimmers need to be at with regards to rip currents. First step is to avoid them. You should also prepare yourself, in advance, for the possibility that a rip current might form. Although every current, body of water and scenario is different, if you do find yourself in a rip current, here are some general actions that may help you find your way to safety.

1. **Remain calm**
If you find yourself in a body of water that is moving, remain calm. The ability to remain calm partly comes from preparation and education. Be aware that if you fear for your safety, you may go into panic and not think logically. Stay calm to allow yourself to think of the next step.

2. **Now act quickly**
The quicker you carry out the following steps to establish the situation you are in, the better.

3. **Breathe**
Keep your mouth clear of the waves and carefully take breaths, avoiding taking water in.

4. **Look around**

Identify what is likely to be feeding the current. Is it water from broken waves working its way back out to sea? Wind? Flash-flooding entering the water? Anything else?

5. **Assess**

Has what you have identified as feeding the current stopped? This may indicate that the current will dissipate. Can you identify the extent of the current you are in? Look for changes in surface texture between where you are, compared to nearby areas of the water, direction of flow and the width of the current.

6. **Move**

Make purposeful movements to swim to safety. If you remain in the current, it may eventually subside, but you will still need to get ashore. Where is your exit point? Or, if you have identified the width of the current and can see areas of water with little or no current, get to one of these. It is common that rip currents are relatively narrow bodies of water, so swimming across them at 90 degrees to the flow can be a fast and effective way to escape their pull.*

---

*   Remember that these tips are general. It is impossible to produce an exact "one size fits all" action plan for every scenario where water and currents are involved and so you must decide what to do and act accordingly to the unique situation in which you find yourself.

Using the waves to escape

In big wave surfing I have found myself in ferocious currents, both in front of waves and in the areas around the waves where water is returning to sea. In night swimming I have taken a technique from big wave surfing to help get back ashore. If I feel that I have been moved beyond where I am comfortable, and the current is pushing me out, I will swim across the current. However, I will also use the waves to help move me to shore either through "bodysurfing" (riding waves with no board) or by simply making myself "big". To do this, I will actively push myself up out of the water into the path of the white water, as waves approach. This allows the wave to push me with it at least for a moment or two. I will repeat this as often as I need to until I'm back closer to shore.

It is important to note that this technique has been useful to me based on my experiences but it is not always appropriate depending on conditions and ability. You should not solely rely upon it or any one technique as a way to get back to shore.

Understanding and recognizing the potential for rip currents and knowing how to escape them is vital for a swimmer. I can understand how someone might think this is a bit over-the-top knowledge for a quick dip in the sea, but it is precisely this kind of detailed knowledge that you will need, when you do not expect it. The sea is never static. It never behaves the same today as it does tomorrow. The conditions may appear identical on paper, but you don't know what sand has moved, for example, since you were last out there. Knowing some of the possibilities is what makes the difference in being able to navigate, go with the flow, fight the flow and be at ease in the water at any given time.

Waves and lulls

There are many different types of waves – open ocean waves, swell, wind swell, local wind-driven waves and probably regional terminology for all the above. Usually, if waves are breaking, it is likely that some of the energy created by the waves turning to white water is moving toward the shore. That's not to say that there may not be other movements in the water too, such as currents below the water, but generally if waves are breaking it is a good indicator that the water flow is toward shore. I like the sound of breaking waves when I'm night swimming because it means if I need to get ashore, I can body surf a wave back to the beach.

It is common for surfers and swimmers to refer to a pause between wave action as a lull. By a lull I mean that a set of waves has broken, and the ocean is catching its breath before sending the next pulse of waves toward shore.

I don't like being out in the dark, open ocean where no waves are breaking. There is very little out there to show me my way. The sound and energy of the surf gives me plenty of signs that I am relatively safe where I am. However, if a lull in this wave action happens, which it will, I can no longer be sure that the water is moving toward shore. In fact, it may be going back out to sea.

The energy from the broken waves will use this pause in the oceans pulse to race back out to sea before the next pulse of waves arrives. It is this lull that, to the untrained eye, may appear to be safer because there are no waves breaking, when, in fact, the water is stealthily rushing back out to sea. If you are not aware of this, then you too could find yourself rushing out to sea with it. So, always be on the lookout for lulls in wave action; it is often a sign that the energy flow is about to change direction. You will know this at night because the sound of the waves will lower or diminish altogether. This flow out to sea can be anything from barely noticeable, to violent and potentially lethal, depending on the local characteristics and weather at the time.

Wind on the water

No one element stands alone. Knowing the effect wind has on your local swim spot can be a huge asset to you as a swimmer. Although wind isn't generated by the water we swim in, the sea's behaviour in relation to the wind can give you clues to what may be happening in the water. When the wind makes contact with the sea, it creates patterns on the surface in the form of tiny little imperfections seemingly rushing across the surface. It could be argued that the safest wind for a swimmer is no wind, but it can be an asset, particularly at night. The wind creates spray and moves water, which can help us with navigation.

Knowing what the wind will be like when you swim is vital. You can get wind forecast information from newspapers and online. I use wetterzentrale.de and windguru.com and both can be used globally.

You should not be in the water if the wind is blowing faster than you can swim against it. If the wind is stronger than 8 kmph (5 mph), you probably won't be able to swim against the water flow it may create.

It is worth remembering that just as the moon, tides, currents and waves all have infinite possibilities in terms of how they behave and interact, the same is true of the wind. The wind direction is often referred to in relation to the compass, but in reality, the wind can come from any direction despite what a forecast might predict. Be aware that if you listen to the wind forecast, "westerly" means it is predicted to *come* from the west. It does not mean it will be blowing *to* the west.

There are many local factors that affect wind direction. You should familiarize yourself with the direction your swim spot faces, and pay attention to how the wind behaves in your local area, becoming familiar with its different directions and speeds. Where I swim, part of the beach has huge basalt cliffs at the water's edge. These cliffs can shelter the water from a strong southerly wind, cause a light westerly wind to swing to the east for minutes at a time, and any wind from the north can cause stones and rocks to fall from the cliff.

Offshore wind

In my opinion, an offshore wind, that is, a wind blowing from the land to the sea, is probably the most dangerous wind for a swimmer, particularly if the wind is strong. An offshore wind can make getting back to shore difficult for an inexperienced swimmer. The same is true of swimming in lakes, loughs/lochs or rivers, but there are usually more options for getting ashore at a point down wind.

Offshore winds can create strong, unpredictable currents that may make it difficult to return to shore,

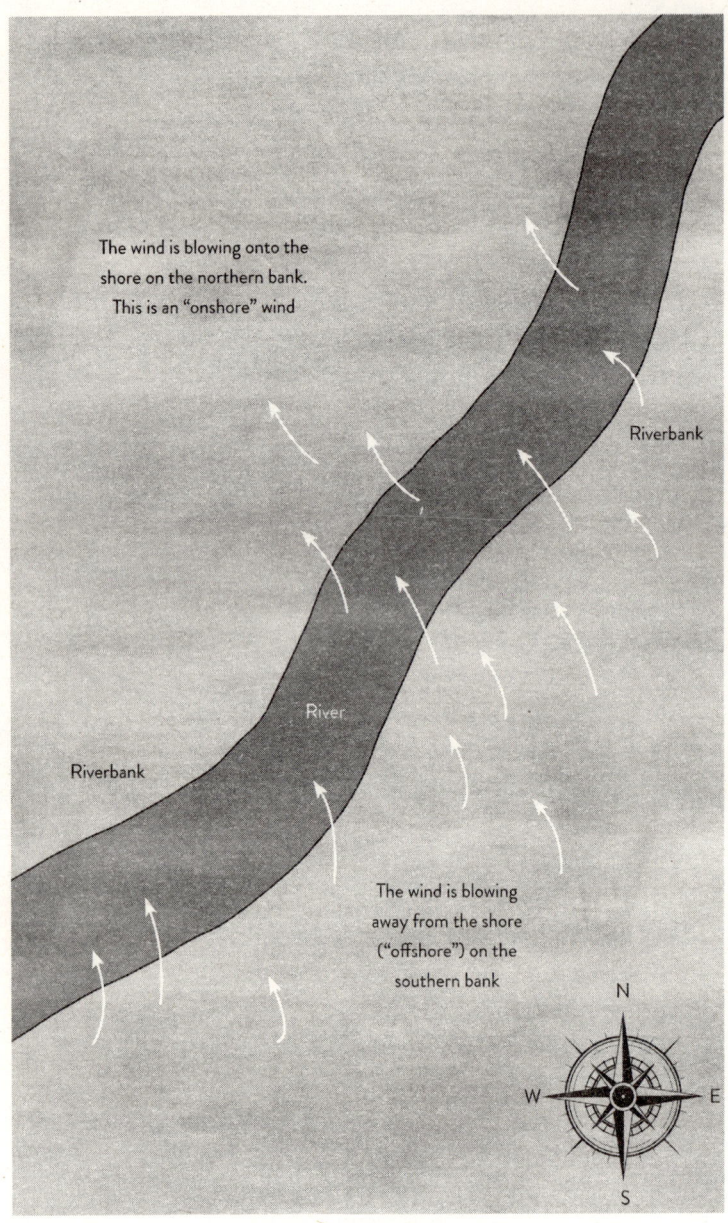

The wind is blowing onto the shore on the northern bank. This is an "onshore" wind

Riverbank

River

Riverbank

The wind is blowing away from the shore ("offshore") on the southern bank

Figure 7: River onshore/offshore wind

especially for swimmers unfamiliar with the area. It is vital to thoroughly consider and apply safety measures if you choose to swim.

Where I swim, the cliffs at one end of the beach can provide shelter in strong offshore winds but only if I am directly below the cliff. If I move ever so slightly away from the cliffs to the east or the west, then the wind reaches the water and becomes dangerous.

In general, I would not recommend swimming any-where in an offshore.

Onshore wind

An onshore wind is usually the safest wind for a swimmer, at most locations. Onshore wind is a wind blowing from the sea to the land. The sea is often choppy in this wind direction because the wind has so much exposure to the water that it can create surface chop and waves. This onshore wind usually helps keep swimmers closer to shore but, as always, do not rule out the possibility of other developments in the water caused by the wind. When the wind has so much exposure to the water it can create currents and waves and push debris and pollution ashore. All these need to be considered, along with any other factors already covered.

Cross-shore wind

This is my favourite wind direction for swimming. If a strong westerly wind blows for long enough at my north-facing swim spot, it can create a very steady flow of water parallel to the beach. That makes swimming much easier and more enjoyable for me. The beach is 16 kilometres

(10 miles) long and curves slightly, meaning that I have the luxury of changing position within my swim spot to benefit from various wind directions.

Like all this ocean-related knowledge, there is no textbook answer to how to handle such a dynamic environment. You need to consider the elements on the day you wish to swim. Tiny pieces of information provided by the elements are your key to enjoying the water safely, even if you only need them once in a blue moon.

Translating the language of the sea

You must spend time reading the conditions presented to you by the sea or the water you plan to swim in, whether day or night. Some may only be identifiable in daylight but knowing of their presence may help you swim more safely at night. Translating what you read in the water's behaviour into information to help you swim, is the key to your safety and enjoyment. You can then choose somewhere to swim that will allow you the best opportunity to enjoy it.

The sea tells a different story in every part of the coast. Different things happen to your swim spot than happen at mine. The signs I read, and how I interpret them, are also different to the signs you will read from the water and how you interpret them.

I encourage you to get to know your local area intimately. I have a few locations within a 20-minute walk of my house that I have known for over 40 years. Although they are all different in terms of location, they are interconnected by the same elements. If there is a strong northerly wind and the surf zone is littered with logs and trees, I swim in a pool called the Monk's Pool.

Near where I live there is a little cove where cold-water dippers go each morning. The Castlerock Mermaids stand and float in knee-to-chest-deep water, among the surf. Their spot is right next to a little stream, some rocks and where the current from the sandbank (see page 47) usually ends. They know the spot intimately and regularly decide when it isn't safe to be swimming, and call off their dip if conditions don't suit. It is that kind of connection and awareness to the location you choose that you need to develop as a swimmer.

A greater power

To know the sea and understand the language it speaks can be far more than a hobby. For many, it is a way of life. The sea can demand that level of commitment from you. We can view the sea as a "god", a real, tangible power on this earth, so great that it commands respect from every living organism. Hear it speak to you through clues left at all stages of the tide and build up intimate knowledge of its personality. Know how it will react to its surroundings when exposed to the elements and be able to translate this language into knowledge, action plans and adaptability. There are countless rivers, oceans and inland bodies of water around the world where the communities regard them as gods, goddesses or have god-like deities associated with the water. From my swim spot I can see a submerged sandbank where the Irish sea god, Manannán mac Lir, is said to be buried. When the sea is raging, plumes of white spray are whipped into the air as waves thrash chaotically over the sandbank, warning water users to stay away.

If you can perceive the water as a force so powerful that it can take you in an instant, then you will adopt the attitude that you only get to enjoy the sea if the sea allows it. This mindset creates the perception that we must always tread carefully and only enter when we have studied its mood. Learn how to identify the mood the water is in, and what is going to affect its behaviour that day, and then you can predict, to some degree, if it is a good time for you to be swimming with it, or not.

CHAPTER 5
BATTLE SUIT

The tide is huge and swelling into the sand dunes. Each wave of surf is eating away at the coast's last line of defence to a broiling, winter sea. Chaotic white water is thrashing and surging from as far as I can see, in the dwindling, afternoon light.

I was nearing the end of my annual charity swim campaign. The campaign represents resilience and persistence in the face of our challenges. The return to the sea each night, to face the unknown, symbolizes that we must keep going in life to overcome whatever it is that life has thrown in our path. Over the past 23 nights, I had swum almost 50 kilometres (30 miles) in some of the most relentless storms I can remember.

Fatigue and self-doubt had found their way into my body and mind. My body was exhausted. The relentless storms had created uncertainty about what the sea had in store for me. I felt mentally drained, and was losing motivation to keep going, despite being so close to the end.

This was not my first time feeling like this after weeks of swimming in the cold nights of winter. I had been here before and so I had prepared for this eventuality happening again. I needed a little motivation to get me amped up and stop letting this slump hold me down. I had one last thing to fall back on to pull me right, something I refer to as the "battle suit". If you are going to explore night swimming, you need to get prepared.

A wetsuit can be the difference in staying home and getting in the water.

The concept of the battle suit originated from my experience in big wave surfing. Big wave surfing often involves last-minute decisions to dash across the globe in the hope of being in the right place at the right time to catch an incoming swell. Sometimes I will drive for seven hours through the night and at other times I will catch a flight to be in the right place for when a swell makes landfall. What may appear as little more than a surfer sliding down the face of a big wave is often only the climactic moment of hours, and often days, of non-stop preparation and travelling.

The anticipation of the big surf leads to sleepless nights, for up to a week in advance. Excitement and adrenaline pulse through my veins, long before I even see the swell arrive at the coast.

All the last-minute stress, planning and preparation culminate in a feeling of relief that I made it to the location on time. A huge dump of energy and adrenaline ensues. This can mean being extremely tired before I even enter the water. It can also allow doubts of my ability to creep in, creating a real psychological battle to get myself out there. I can remember numerous times, standing shivering, before entering some of the biggest seas ever recorded. I wasn't cold from feeling the atmospheric temperature, but from being drained psychologically and emotionally from all the build-up to that moment.

It is in those moments that the battle suit became a necessity. I needed something to help me face the water and my mind. If I couldn't win the mental battle, then I wouldn't get the chance to go to battle in the surf. To be a big wave surfer requires confidence in the face of the ocean's almighty power and unpredictability. The same is true of night swimming. Confidence is key but always remember it must be paired with caution and respect for the water.

Be prepared

Over many years I learned that I needed to simplify every part of the process. I began to pay great attention to what I wore and how I looked. I had a custom-built wetsuit made by a company in Cornwall. I took 21 precise measurements around my body, and the tailor expertly shaped every panel and line of stitching to fit snuggly to my contours. Just like water forms perfectly around me, the wetsuit would do the same. Putting it on flicks a confidence switch in my mind when I need it most.

I ordered the suit in the colour red for three reasons. Red symbolizes sacrifice, passion and courage: all the elements required to overcome dangerous situations. Being red also meant that I would be easily identifiable in a wild sea if something were to go wrong. The colour was also a nod to my big wave mission in the early 2000s: Project Red.

Through each step of suiting up, I feel myself getting into battle mode. Every tug of the neoprene, as I pull it over my skin, feels like I am adding a layer of protection, an invincible shield against all doubt and negativity. As I haul the hood over my head, I shed worry and fortify my mind. I feel like a gladiator – I look and feel big, strong and powerful. All the things the mind needs to feel in the face of the biggest waves on earth. The suit made me feel so powerful, taking me into another realm of ability, regardless of what I faced in the ocean or in my mind!*

I had another suit made for ocean paddleboarding, with specifically placed panels for wind protection, thinner panels for flexibility, and others for warmth. I had another made for night swimming that had more flexible neoprene and a different chest zip pattern to keep the suit as close to me as possible and not flush water in whilst I swam through raging surf.

For you, your battle suit might be a wonderfully comfortable swimming costume, changing robe, a special towel and swim cap. You can buy second-hand wetsuits, or borrow one, to help you take those first steps.

Night swimming can often mean getting home late at night and wanting to go straight to bed. The idea of removing our swimming gear from the van or car can seem like a chore at that time of night. It often gets left in a bucket overnight, in the cold and damp. However, the next day, when we want to go in the water again, we are punished for the laziness of the night before by having to put on a soaking icy wetsuit pulled from a bucket of water! The excitement of getting into the water again is powerful enough for some to overcome the feeling of a miserable-looking wetsuit. But, I have seen people cave in to the thought of putting a wet, sandy wetsuit on, and forgo going in the water. So, take that time to hang up your wetsuit after a swim, in a warm, dry room.

---

* While my wetsuit and safety equipment provide an added sense of protection, they are not a substitute for strong swimming skills and safety awareness. There are many dynamic risks in the water and having good equipment has helped add confidence to my ability.

If you would like to develop your very own version of a battle suit, here are some things to consider:

- **Safety.** Your wetsuit should have safety features that make you feel like you have back-up, that you are not alone in what you are doing. I have a Hi-Viz whistle and light attached to my wetsuit, beside my mouth.

- **Functionality.** Your wetsuit should function better than any other equipment you have. Putting it on should bring you a new level of physical, mental and emotional ability. My night swimsuit is 6 mm (¼ in) thick, so it is warm, and offers some buoyancy should I need it. It is a snug fit to stop water getting in.

- **Colour.** All-black wetsuits mean you are difficult to spot in the water. Choose colours so you can be seen. The colour of your wetsuit could also mean something to you. This could be connected to your family name or country of birth, giving you a feeling of pride and connection to who you are when you wear your battle suit.

The battle suit as a motivator

Your battle suit may not be a wetsuit. For you, it might be a swimsuit, board shorts or a bikini. Maybe it is the clothes you wear to work every day or your make-up. Your battle suit is any preparation you do for the tougher times in life. Whatever it is, you should choose it with purpose and intention. The feeling that it creates is the underlying benefit.

I learned that my wetsuit makes me feel like a superhero; it makes me feel like I'm getting dressed to go on stage as a rock star! It helps me shake off any low mood and reminds me of who I am, why I'm going out there, and what I am capable of. The immense psychological boost takes me to a high state of readiness. The physical empowerment it brings creates mental empowerment and motivation even in my darkest of moments. I believe that when I treat equipment with the utmost respect, it delivers the same respect to me.

Your body is your battle suit

Our body carries us through our life. It houses our mind, soul and spirit. We rely upon our body to deal with life's daily stresses and often, with little to no specific attention to detail on our part, it does a commendable job. But when things get tough, and dark times settle into our lives, it can manifest physically. When I used to feel stress in my life, my default was to neglect my diet and exercise. This could spiral into physical decline, when really I needed to be at my best.

I began to realize that my training had always focused on surfing, swimming or something related to the sea. I train to perform and survive in huge, wild seas. But one day I realized that, even though I was very capable in the water and had learned to thrive in that environment, I had neglected other areas of life. I needed to develop a battle suit for those too. To enhance my overall fitness and have a solid reserve of physical ability I brought these into my life:

- **Weight-training.** To build strength.

- **Martial arts.** To learn quick, logical thinking and self-defence skills.

- **Flexibility exercises/yoga.** To help with muscle growth and joint movement,

- **Endurance.** To know that I can keep going. Pool swimming, hiking, cycling . . . whatever you enjoy.

By including these, I added a more general fitness to my regime. This made me feel much more capable as a human being, rather than simply good in the water.

Being your own lifeguard

The concept of a battle suit extends to other kit we use as swimmers. Having the correct gear to suit you and your swimming is crucial to having a wonderful time in the water, but also being able to act confidently to avoid, or escape, a bad situation. And that also applies to life. As children, we are taught that the police and fire rescue will help us, and the lifeguard will swim out and rescue us if we are in trouble in the water. It isn't until we are older that we realize that these are people just like us. They have fears, emotions and courage to do what they do in the face of danger. The services that provide these people in our times of need are often running on stretched resources, yet if the public call, they will endeavour to race to the aid of someone in distress. I believe we all have a responsibility to ourselves and our communities to be capable of looking after ourselves, without needing to burden the emergency services, unless necessary. Through foresight and planning, we can do our best to help ourselves out of a bad situation or avoid one occurring. However, while it's important to be as self-sufficient as possible, never hesitate to call for professional help if the situation requires it. Always prioritize your safety and wellbeing, and recognize when you need assistance from trained professionals.

In my opinion, you should be 100 per cent competent and capable of swimming without the need for devices, equipment and tools in the water. When I began night swimming, I simply used my wetsuit and nothing else. However, there are items that should at least be considered as an extension of us in the water, there for peace of mind or be there in an emergency. Remember that none of these devices or tools are a substitute for good water knowledge, swimming ability and sensible decisions before, during and after swimming.

- **Battery-powered light/Emergency light.** I have never used lights to see my way through the dark. Lights in the surf zone disorientate me. There is too much glare from the white water. But it can be helpful to wear one so my friends can locate me. You can buy waterproof lights and place them on your head, back, helmet or wrist. I use a high-powered LED light kept inside my radio pouch, which when lit, glows brightly and can be visible from a distance.

- **Impact vest.** Where I swim, there is a chance that something might hit me in the water, such as tree branches, logs, even items from shipwrecks. My impact vest is a thick foam vest covered in neoprene. I use them in big wave surfing in some situations, so am well used to swimming with one on. They give a little protection should anything hit me underwater, and they provide a little buoyancy and extra warmth, too. It is a simple thing to wear over a wetsuit and is a good safety choice to consider. Be aware that many impact vests appear like flotation vests, but they aren't.

- **Flotation vest/lifejacket.** I don't use lifejackets because they can be dangerous in the surf as they don't allow penetration of the water to get below breaking waves, but this is something you need to make your own choices on, depending on where you swim and your ability. Choose one that is rated with the correct newton buoyancy rating for your weight.

- **Dry bag.** I swim with a waterproof, and luminous dry bag. In this I keep a walkie-talkie and emergency light.

- **Walkie-talkie and whistle.** It is important that we can communicate from the sea to the land or between other swimmers and water users. I use a combination of waterproof walkie-talkies and whistles to communicate with people ashore. This was a game-changer for me, making me feel at ease in the water and satisfying others who were concerned for my safety. Walkie-talkies are small, inexpensive and easily replaced if they are lost or damaged by saltwater, which can happen if the pressure in the surf breaks the seals on your dry bag. You can get walkie-talkies with lights, too. I sometimes wear one on my arm, if not using a bag.

- **VHF radio.** I sometimes take a waterproof radio. It is set for instant access to my local coastguard (channel 16).

- **Cell phone.** Depending on where you swim, a cell phone might be sufficient and can be stored inside a wetsuit or bag (you can buy waterproof phones and cases).

- **Knife.** I keep a blunt-nosed knife in a sheath up the ankle of my wetsuit. It is a simple and easy tool to carry that, although highly unlikely I ever need it, it could help me escape a stray rope or fishing net, for example. If you plan to carry one, be aware of local laws about blade dimensions and reasons of carry, as they differ across the globe.

- **EPIRB** (Emergency Position Indicating Radio Beacon). One of the smartest tools you can use as a swimmer. It provides rescue services with your location via satellites, so they can find you very quickly, should the need arise. I have never used one, but many kayakers, boaters, etc. use them. You could speak to local rescue organizations about the most useful ones for your area, if you plan to get one.

USING A WHISTLE

I have a waterproof whistle tied to my wetsuit hood for easy access. In most conditions this is of limited use to me because the roar of the sea overpowers the sound, but when it is calmer I use it every 30 seconds or so, to let anyone supporting me from the shore know that I'm ok. It is easier to use than the radio.

Water quality and pollution

Being aware of what may be in the water when we swim is crucial to protecting our health. Some water may have pollutants in it consistently, and some water may have pollutants or debris at certain stages of the tide or season. This should be considered at your swim spot and, if necessary, you will need to postpone swims until the water is clean again. A river feeds into the sea where I swim, which can make the water extremely dirty at times as there are sewage pumping stations and industrialization areas that feed into the river. It has become a serious issue that is leading to protest and government intervention to try and tackle it.

There are also multiple streams, waterfalls and an estuary near where I swim, all of which influence the water. Often the water from the waterfalls is crystal clear, but in heavy rainfall the water can become murky as sediment from the fields is washed into the surf

All along the coast, in rivers and lakes, wherever you swim, you will be exposed to different levels of pollutants. With observation, speaking to locals, following online alerts, etc., you will learn where it is safest to be in the water and have a deeper sense of connection to your local environment.

In the USA, the Government Accountability Office (GAO) states that: "Over the past 50 years, the nation's water quality and drinking water have improved, but threats to water quality and safety remain. For example, the Environmental Protection Agency (EPA) and the states have identified almost 70,000 water bodies nationwide that do not meet water quality standards."

Industrialization, tourism and farming can lead to pollution, sewage and algae in the water. Blue-green algae (cyanobacteria) can cause irritation of the skin and respiratory problems, so swimming in it isn't a good idea. At my swim spot it is such an issue that, from August to October, it can be seen staining the sands green when the tide pulls back. On two occasions in the past year, I have left the water because of it.

The rivers bring fallen trees and other debris into the sea too. The flow from the river into the sea here is so prominent and strong that it leaves a huge scar on the water's surface. It is identifiable by the surface of the water being obviously more chaotic and choppier and stained by peat. The riverbed has a peat base and so the water is like a brown iodine in colour. There is a brown edge to the flow of the water, which is so clearly defined next to the saltwater that you could pilot a boat around the edge of it and never cross into the other side. It is visible for miles in some conditions. If you swim near an estuary, look out for a similar pattern on the water after heavy rain, or very low tides, when more water is drawn out of the estuary into the sea.

I do not swim in strong northerly wind as I feel the risk of being hit by something in the water or by some form of pollution is more likely. My swim spot faces north, and so a north wind pushes the water from the rivers and the sea back toward shore. At your swim spot you should find out what wind will do the same and if there is any likelihood that what it may bring ashore – from the opposite bank of the river or lake, or from the sea – is potentially of any harm to you. But it may be that the opposite is true. Everywhere is different and you can only find out by paying attention and connecting as deeply as possible with the water where you swim.

Microplastics are another issue in our water. I took part in a UK-wide survey in 2021 which involved me collecting water samples at the estuaries near my swim spot. The results showed that some of the worst microplastic pollution in the UK was here, on my doorstep. The prevalence of microplastics is down to industrial pollution, over-use of plastics globally, and poor recycling. Much of it ends up in rivers, lakes and the sea.

If you do feel unwell after a swim, consult your doctor promptly. Good planning around tides and local weather leads can help mitigate the potential for any risk to your health.

Be in tune with where you are swimming so that you know and recognize when the water is not safe to be in. Be ready to alter your swim plans accordingly. Get used to recognizing changes in the water colour, clarity and texture. Notice around the edges or on the beach if there is scum, algae blooms, etc. There may be an unusual smell too. But be aware that not all pollution will be picked up by your senses and to use local knowledge, reports and any other sources of information you can to keep yourself safe.

Wildlife

If you plan to swim anywhere, you should know what, or who, you are sharing the water with. Locals, swimming groups, fishermen, surfers and other regulars in a particular area will have knowledge of the types of sea creatures there. Where I swim, wildlife isn't much of a concern, and it can be wonderful to share the space with them. In my local area the porpoises always cruise by at dusk. Sometimes I only see one, but often there are two swimming parallel to the shoreline with one slightly ahead of the other. Seals appear too, but if they do, it is usually out just behind the surf, not close to shore. Unlike the porpoises, they don't appear to be swimming in any direction and will stop and inspect! There are a couple of little seals that seem to follow me from time to time, their heads silhouetted by the distant streetlights. As far as I know, they only ever come to check me out, and they don't come very close.

We also have basking sharks and occasional orca sightings in spring, but not much else. I don't think any of these are a threat to me, but in some parts of the world, swimming at night may not be an option if you have sharks or other predators in the water. Australia, Florida, California, South Africa and many more places have sharks, as well as less dangerous sea life such as manatees, dolphins and turtles. Some beaches in Durban

Figures 8, 9 and 10: Shark, seal and conger eel

and Sydney have shark nets to prevent them coming into the swimming area, so although some potential threats may exist, many popular spots have already taken precautions. Some of the harbours here in Northern Ireland have large conger eels but they don't come into my swim spot. I have swum at night in Ballintoy harbour in County Antrim, which is so well known for conger eels that there is a local tale about a giant one taking someone from the harbour, across the channel to Scotland! I didn't encounter it, though.

It is vital that before you enter water you always familiarize yourself with the local wildlife, consult locals, check for official advisories and stay aware of the creatures you may encounter.

Your onshore team

As much as night swimming is wonderful for us, and we take every precaution to make sure we can do it safely and enjoy it, we must not do so without considering how it may appear to an onlooker, another water user, someone fishing, etc. I have taken this aspect as seriously as every other part of night swimming, as I feel it has serious potential for putting others at risk. No matter how experienced, knowledgeable and competent one might be, an onlooker may not be aware of that. They may see someone enter the water after dark and have grave concerns for their safety, but also their mental state. This could lead to a call to the emergency services, leading to others taking risks and applying resources to make sure the person entering the water is ok. This is one of the reasons I almost always have someone with me on the

Figure 11: Onshore team (viewed from swimmer's perspective)

beach. Not that I feel I will ever need help in the water, but it is to give anyone who may see me a person to speak to, or at least to see from a distance that someone is there.

Being conscious of how others may perceive what you are doing will make it more enjoyable for all involved.

My friends that do land support for me on my swims are mostly frontline emergency response professionals: paramedic, ambulance crew, police, ex-army, a lifeguard and a few others. They are geared up with a full medical kit, ropes, flippers, wetsuits and of course, hot chocolate!

Always check in with someone on shore before entering the water, and make sure they have the means to contact emergency services if necessary. Clear communication is a fundamental part of water safety.

Know where you are

Always have a swim plan before you set off. Write it down or tell someone. Doing this is a great way of confirming to yourself that you have made educated decisions on what you are doing, have thought it through based on the knowledge and experience you have gained, and you are therefore using that to swim safely. Be ready to continually reassess your plan. Water environments are dynamic, and your safety depends on being adaptable and vigilant. Be prepared to communicate effective information that can assist those that may come to your aid, should the need arise. Imagine the scenario where you had to communicate your location to someone over radio. You should know the coordinates of where you enter the water, at the very least.

Swimming in groups

Night swimming can be a magical experience with others. In the winter months I often see the cold-water dippers from my village on the beach before sunrise. They refuse to let the light dictate if they get their daily fix of saltwater or not. A local swim group in Bettystown, on the east coast of Ireland, recently swam in beautiful still conditions at night. They carried small candles with them into the water and had a great time marking the end of summer, bobbing around in the shallows. Swimming with others can also be a great way to use local knowledge and experience to help make judgements on water conditions and to look out for each other.

Emergency back-up

I always prepare for self-sufficiency and self-rescue through preparation, knowledge and experience, but have the means of contacting rescue services should the need to do so arise (see pages 82–4). Find out what rescue organizations exist where you plan to swim before you step into the water. In the UK, HM Coastguard answers emergency calls from people needing assistance on the water. In the USA, the US Coast Guard handle similar scenarios. I, personally, have never relied upon them and certainly wouldn't consider them if planning any kind of mission, swim, surf session, etc. It is highly unreasonable, in my opinion, to be factoring in charity or public-funded rescue services into our own personal adventures! You should also remember that rescue organizations may not have as much experience as you in the water you are swimming in, and so relying on them putting themselves at risk to rescue you from your swim is unfair.

Be the best lifeguard that you can possibly be for yourself. The best lifeguards do the least rescues – that is because they can foresee the dangers and take steps to prevent them. Never be so arrogant or narrow-minded to not have several means of communication to reach rescue services should you need them.

And that goes for life too. There is no shame in asking for help when you are struggling. A different perspective from someone else's point of view is sometimes all we need to see past obstacles and shine light into a dark place.

Your battle suit for life

Taking the concept of a battle suit into other areas of life is a great way of helping us navigate through periods when we may be struggling to keep going. It is our approach to life that makes us more relaxed in the face of adversity.

You may have done like I have and created a battle suit for occasions when you need a boost to perform and feel at your best. We feel motivated and breathe a little boost of energy back into our mind and body. An internal battle suit is, in some ways, a by-product of the physical, but we can also develop and grow it in other ways to help us overcome adversity in life.

Hoping that we will never face dark times is not a sustainable solution or a suitable way to live life. We must use our experience to make things better in the future. We must not live in fear of something terrible coming that we may not be able to handle, but rather, prepare ourselves for the eventuality of it and be able to act quickly. Ordinary life events such as relationships, finances, illness, etc. can throw us off-course. Or it could be extraordinary events that we could never have foreseen happening in our lives, that we have no knowledge or understanding of, until faced with them.

It is possible to get through life having enough stamina to carry out daily activities, but what happens if you need to act quickly? What happens if yours or someone else's life depends on you? Wouldn't it be great to be your own hero, and for your family and friends, when they hit dark times in life and need a strong person to hold them up?

You can be all of those things by taking time to develop your own battle suit for life that you can step into when times are tough, to help you deal confidently with the unknown. So do your best to create your own battle suit that allows you to swim through situations and unknown waters with confidence, and through doing so, you can help others keep their heads above water, too.

There is often no way to predict what turn life might take. It can be just as useful to not spend our lives trying to forecast what may or may not be coming next. I believe it is important to have a healthy balance between being prepared to swim through the dark waters that at times appear in our lives and also being able to go with the flow of life and trust that things will work out.

The sudden loss of my father in 2003 threw me into the darkest waters of my life that, only now, over 20 years later, have I learned how to swim through. I spent many years keeping myself afloat as I attempted to find my way through the waves and raging currents of bereavement. It was the biggest shock my system has ever had . . . so far.

I recently realized that my concept of "swimming through the dark waters" has come from this event in my life. My father died of a heart attack shortly after swimming. He swam every day and used it as exercise and to destress from life. I wonder if, subconsciously, I have taken to swimming so intensely through seeing my dad use it in his life.

The thing I did to survive that time of my life was to build extreme belief in myself. It coincided with my pursuit of big wave surfing and so the two went hand-in-hand. The fact I was powering forward into the sea in the biggest waves on earth, while handling loss and adopting new responsibilities within the family as the eldest son, no doubt had a combined effect on me that kept me feeling in control despite being anything but.

I felt I needed to have the reserves of uncompromising ability of the mind and body should I ever be faced with such scenarios again, in other walks of life.

I took the psychological training I had used in my surfing and adapted it to suit life. I wrote affirmations in the morning and before bed, placing notes on my wall. I did weight-training and martial arts for my self-development. The more I could learn and grow myself, the better I felt.

I have rarely had to draw upon my battle suit in other walks of life, but there's no doubt that the knowledge that I am capable and ready is a huge motivator and driver for me. It will be for you, too, if you decide to dedicate time and energy to building a reserve of mental and emotional capacity to overcome the dark times that inevitably come in life.

Giving time to self-development has led me to feel invincible at times and rise above many petty situations that may have otherwise drawn me in. The knowledge and power in knowing that you are confident to at least attempt to handle any given situation, without the need to call upon someone else, is hugely empowering.

The battle suit does not need to be too specific. What you wear, the tools, devices and back-ups you have, the friends that stand by you and the knowledge you have acquired, are all part of your battle suit. By building resources, experience and knowledge into your life, you prepare yourself to be able to self-rescue, to help others and have confidence in doing so.

CHAPTER 6
FINDING YOUR WAY

I surfaced from the dark silence into a wild winter's night. It was December, and the coast was being thrashed by the full brunt of a storm. I paused swimming and grabbed my radio and hoped the next wave wouldn't take the radio from me. "First waterfall, first waterfall." A crackle, then my friend Denise's voice came out of the dark: "Received. First waterfall, first waterfall." The next wave hit as I fumbled to get the radio back on my arm whilst holding my breath in the dark below the wave. I surfaced, took a breath and broke into front crawl. Stroke after stroke, wave after wave, breath after breath, I continued along the coast. The fresh water from the waterfall clashes with the briny North Atlantic, trying to hold onto its identity, refusing to give up as the Atlantic swamps it. The tumultuous fight between the two forces causes turmoil in the water. Waves break harder, the undertow pushing into the oncoming waves as if trying to hold them back. I finally break through the unsettled energy and continue with the predominant flow to the east. The wind is westerly, the swell raging out of the dark North Atlantic, and the flow steadily pushes to the east. As wild and out of control as this might sound, for me, the conditions were perfect.

Radio silence

On the shoreline, Denise was in complete darkness, dressed head-to-toe in wet weather gear, isolated in the driving rain. Our pace kept synchronized through continual communication of where each other was.

As soon as I was in line with the second waterfall cascading over the dark cliff edge onto the beach, I radioed her again: "Second waterfall, second waterfall." Knobs of rock, church spires and streetlights break the peak of the cliffs and dunes, giving me waypoints to check in and to help navigate my way through the dark night.

I continued to swim through the turbulent sea. Despite the surface appearing chaotic, there is a rhythm to the water when it is like that. These waves have travelled for hundreds of miles before breaking on the shallow sandbanks around me. During that journey across the Atlantic, they march in order, and although the wind whips them into a frenzy, they pulse across the shallows, allowing me to tune in so acutely that my breathing flows with my strokes and the passing of each wave overhead.

Denise is waiting, listening intently for me to check in. Despite the wild conditions, Denise and many other friends insist on being there for me. They cannot see me, have almost no idea where I am, but through a combination of trust and some very simple systems we can keep in contact. Some that walk in the darkness will keep a light on, constantly shining at their feet, so I can see them. Some don't like attention being drawn to them in isolation on the beach and prefer to go unseen, unless they need to attract my attention. These are the people you need to find in life. You don't need many people; you just need good ones. You need them to want to face down any storm, any dark winter's night and walk through life with you. But we must be careful not to put ourselves or them at risk of any danger in doing so. I started this night swimming to escape people during the pandemic in 2020, but in doing so, in the darkness, I found some of the best friends I've ever had.

But, as I swim, I know in my heart that, despite everyone's best intentions, my survival in this world is my responsibility. I keep swimming. With every roll of my body, as I pull myself through the water, I'm mimicking life. Wave after wave, I keep swimming, and we must all do this to survive. Know that others are there but be able to survive on our own.

"Fifth street light, fifth street light." No response. I wondered if Denise spoke while I was underwater. "Denise, fifth street light, fifth street light." This has never happened before. Is she ok? I know Denise carries a personal alarm as she walks in the dark. I listen as best I could through the wind and the crashing surf, and squint toward shore, between waves, hoping to see a glimpse of her. Nothing. She was gone and to her, so was I.

I prefer to be stealthy in the water, not attracting any undue concern from any potential onlooker that might see me and worry for my safety, but this situation called for me to turn on my safety light. I blew my safety whistle, and tried the radio again. The white froth on the surface of the water reflected the light all around, instantly blinding me to my surroundings. It is easier to swim with no light on the water than that glare, but I had no choice, I needed her to see me in case she too was trying to call me and getting no response. Still nothing and no light shone back.

I bodysurfed toward the beach until I could stand up in the shallows. I shouted "Denise!" Suddenly, the radio crackled. "Sorry, Al, I accidentally turned the volume down." In the wild weather, Denise had accidentally hit the volume, and was wondering why I hadn't checked in!

This serves as a reminder that, despite best efforts, it is impossible to foresee every eventuality that may arise in or around the water!

Finding our own way

When we go through dark times in life, it is easy to get so focused on potential disaster scenarios that we lose rational thinking. In that moment, out in the sea, my brain ran wild with all the things that may have happened to Denise. It didn't cross my mind that something so trivial may have happened.

No matter how well prepared we think we are in life, we can sometimes let our minds take over and lead us into dark places, through worry, panic and irrational thoughts.

Night swimming has taught me to be present and read situations both in the water and in life. Being able to foresee potential trouble is a skill developed through experience, and we owe it to ourselves, and those around us, to be prepared even if we never need to draw upon it.

Finding our way in life is a unique and individual journey. Despite our paths crossing, no two of us walk the same route. We don't often know what lies ahead, despite our best attempts to control our futures. In every moment, we put one foot in front of the other as the environment around us pushes and pulls.

The further we go through life, the more in tune we become with it. We learn how to identify obstacles in our way, gaining more control and beginning to carve the path for ourselves.

I use a variety of ways to find my way in the dark, but most of all I rely upon experience. Experience is the one thing no one can buy. We must go through the process of acquiring it. Experience of the sea, in all her moods, dwells in every cell of my body. Experience is earned, through exposure to something and time spent immersed in it. The more time I have spent in my swim spot, the more experience that flows into my body, allowing me to navigate the waters in any given day or night. I spent years of time in the water at my spot during daylight long before venturing out there after dark. I have become part of the environment there in doing so. The time spent surfing, swimming, paddling and walking with my dog there has led to a deep awareness of the surroundings and my place within them. By committing yourself to a lifestyle around the water, you could also become a part of the environment around you.

Celestial navigation

It is an amazing feeling being below the stars while night swimming; it takes the experience of being in the water to another level of intensity. On the rare occasion when the sky is so clear that stars are visible here in Ireland, it can feel like a magical experience.

I can see the Plough constellation where I swim. In some parts of the world it is known as the "Big Dipper" or "Saucepan"; just think – when you are out there swimming, we might be looking at the same stars. When

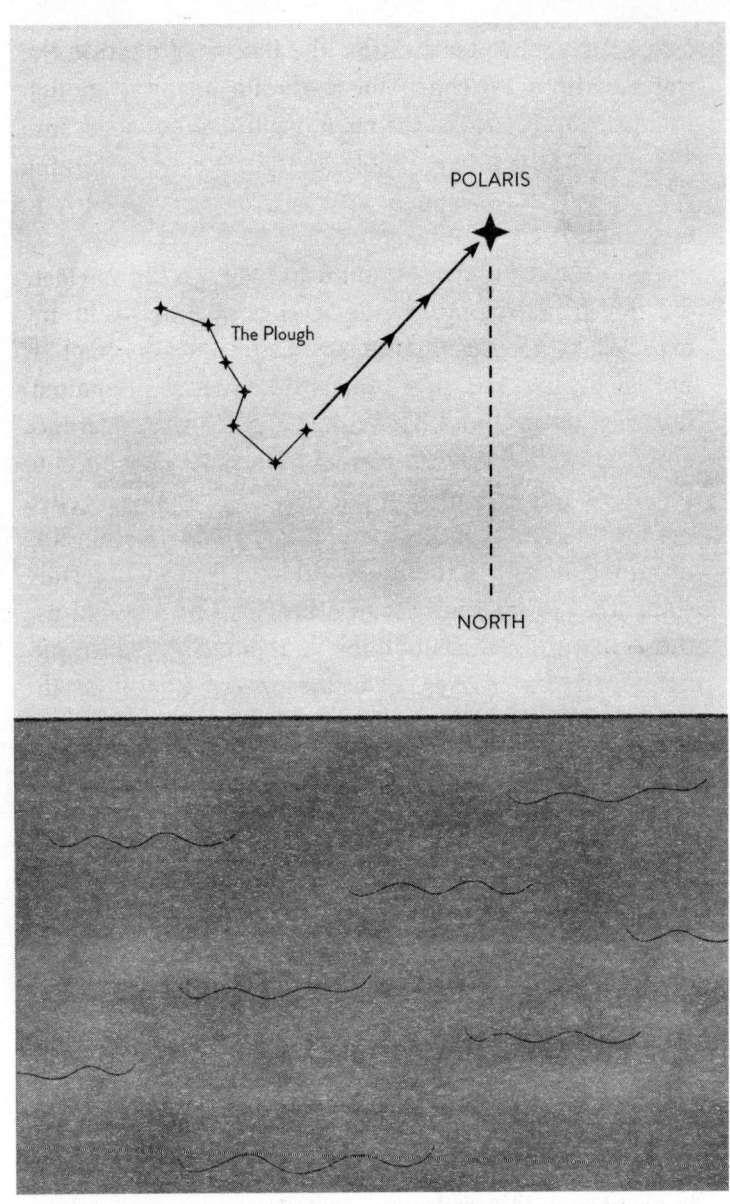

Figure 12: The star Polaris points north when viewed from the Northern Hemisphere

I swim in the winter months, the Plough sits out to the north, helping me check due north. For me, it is enough to know the Plough is sitting above the horizon because I am swimming perpendicular to it. If you are swimming at a different location, you might use the pattern to determine due north.

I wouldn't advise solely on using the stars to navigate for night swimming. While it is a nice idea, in my experience, relying on the sky being clear enough is not worth the risk, when many other more permanent features exist on shore. They are a handy point of reference and another thing which brings a deeper connection to the world around us, but they should never be relied upon exclusively for any form of navigation. Depending on where you are in the world, you will see certain stars more prominently than others and you should use those if they work better for your area. For example, in the southern hemisphere, the pattern known as the "Southern Cross" is prominent in the sky.

Navigating by landmarks

Navigators on ships are often referred to as pilots. Among other techniques, they use fixed visual points of reference to guide a ship through channels, traffic, estuaries, etc. I use a similar system with night swimming, learned from Big Wave Surfing. I set off with the knowledge of ocean charts to hand, but often I use fixed points of reference ashore such as trees and houses to triangulate my position.

Even if I am a mile out to sea, it is rare that no land is visible, so this technique usually works. If you look at lighthouses and churches on the coast, they are often

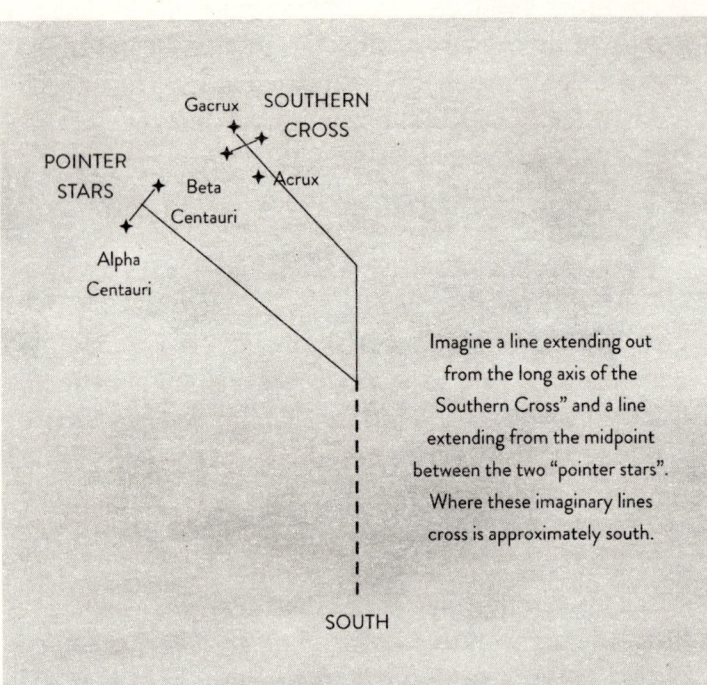

Gacrux

SOUTHERN CROSS

POINTER STARS

Beta Centauri

Acrux

Alpha Centauri

Imagine a line extending out from the long axis of the Southern Cross" and a line extending from the midpoint between the two "pointer stars". Where these imaginary lines cross is approximately south.

SOUTH

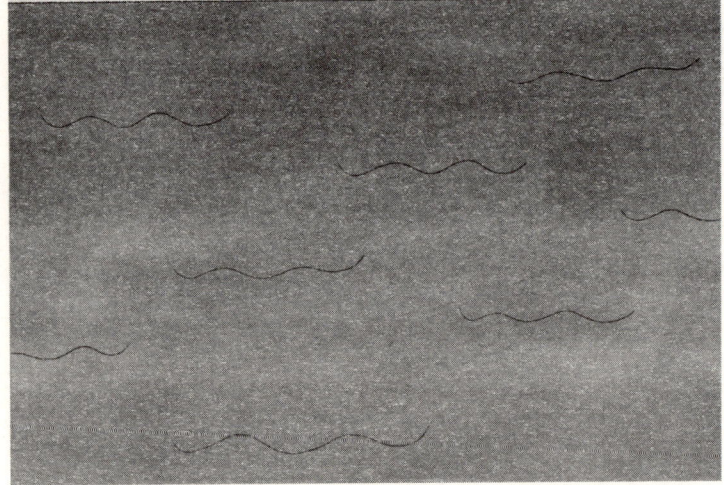

Figure 13: The Southern Cross points to the south when viewed from the Southern Hemisphere.

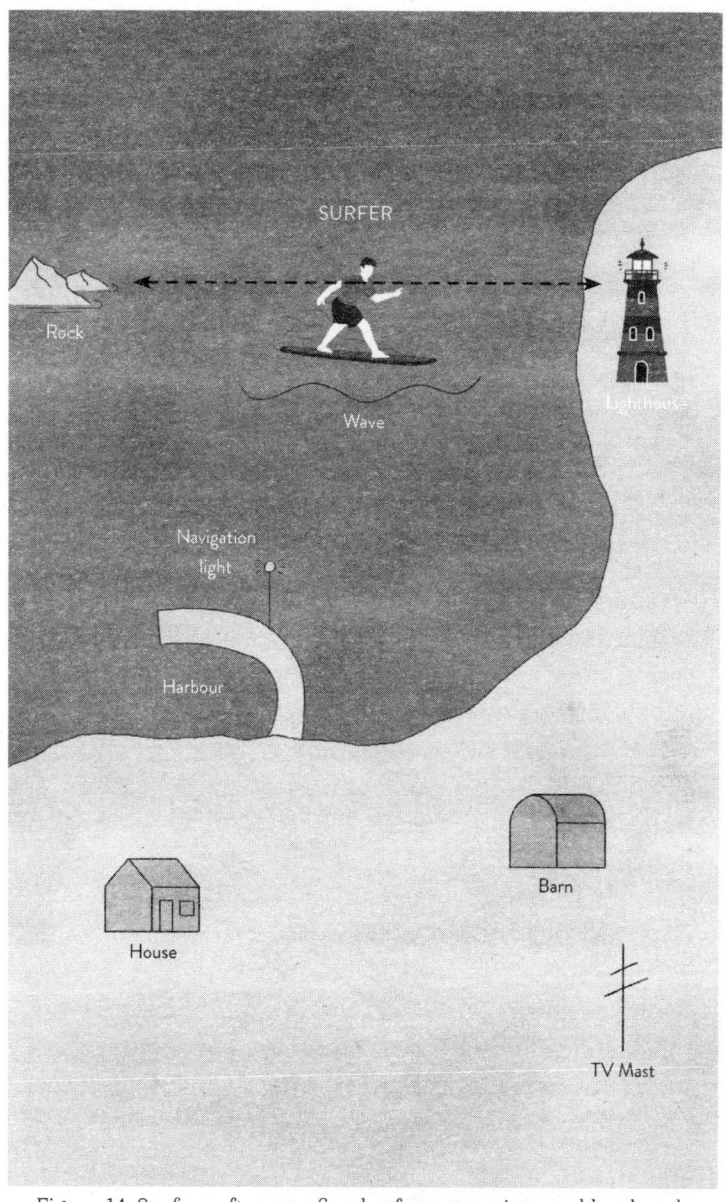

SURFER

Rock

Lighthouse

Wave

Navigation
light

Harbour

Barn

House

TV Mast

Figure 14: Surfers often use fixed reference points and landmarks to position themselves in the water.

painted white so that they are visible to sailors. Look at ocean charts and you will often see churches noted with clear lines of sight from various points marked.

When you begin swimming at night, walk along your swim spot in the evening, and note all the obvious features you can see. It could be a building, a sand dune top, pier, streetlights, etc. Some are always visible, and some are weather dependent, so it is useful to have many. You can then correlate areas of the water to these markers. For example, a church spire marks an area of the water that I know to have difficult currents at almost all tides. I know that once I am near the church spire, the currents would begin to show. The same idea works for knowing how far out in the water I am by using two lights on a nearby pier. One is at the end, and one roughly halfway along it.

This level of knowledge is what you need, long before you venture into the water after dark. You should never allow yourself to become unsure of where you are. Landmarks can be useful points of reference but they shouldn't be used in isolation to establish position or route. Always cross reference them with as many other indicators as possible.

Navigating by water temperature

At my swim spot, freshwater flows into the sea, and is much colder than the sea. The water temperature from the freshwater waterfalls can help me know exactly where I am. If the flow is strong enough compared to the sea, it is possible to notice the definite change in temperature at that section of my swim.

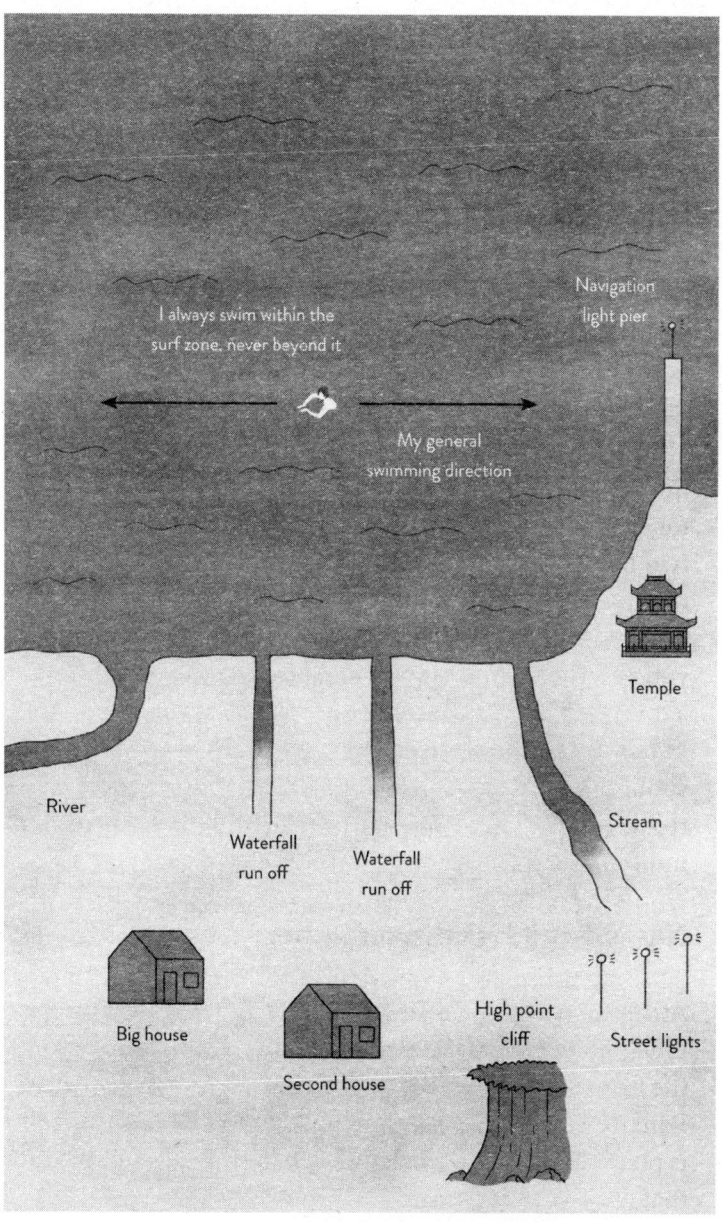

Figure 15: My points of reference when I swim

I sometimes swim in the Monk's Pool at the mouth of the River Bann. In some stages of the tide, it is pure seawater and in others, river water. I remember swimming there one night, with snow on the rocks at sea level, and the water completely still, apart from my wake as I stroked through the water. It was the coldest I have ever been. If I didn't keep swimming, my hands froze up.

You may discover some other local anomaly or characteristics that help you to navigate through your swim spot. In winter, the sea is warmer than the freshwater rivers, estuaries and loughs, but in summer, the opposite is true. The difference is so obvious at times that even if it was pitch dark, I would know where the river water was meeting the sea.

Water temperature can be useful in some circumstances, but it should never be the sole indicator of your position. Always cross-reference temperature changes with visual cues and your general sense of location.

Using your hearing

The sound of water moving can help with navigation, depending on where you are. Maybe you swim in a tranquil pool of water enclosed by rocks and there is nothing but complete silence other than your movement splashing through the water. Swimming in sea and rivers tends to be noisier, and sound can be a great addition to your knowledge.

At my swim spot, the sounds I hear are usually constant waves, and that means I'm within the surf zone as I swim along the beach. I continually monitor the rise and fall of the sound of waves and water around me and cross check all my reference points to be sure where I am. There are also rocks and a large concrete pier in the water, and waves hitting them can be loud and powerful, booming in the darkness, clearly informing me that I am near them.

GPS navigation

You can buy watches and devices to help with navigation. You can also get apps for your phone. Personally, I don't use any of these. I prefer to keep my mind focused on the water around me, rather than rely on a third-party view of what I am doing. However, they can be an asset for some swimmers and locations, so do consider these but do not rely solely on them as they are an addition, not a substitute, for any other safety equipment or techniques, or situational awareness.

I do wear a GPS-enabled watch to track my swims. This allows me to look at my swim in hindsight and see how the water moved me during my swim.

Night swimming safely is like a huge jigsaw puzzle. You must have all the pieces in the box, or you won't be able to see the full picture. With night swimming, you need to use all the pieces to build up a complete view of where you are swimming and how you are going to do it safely. This is completely unique to you and your chosen location and so you must learn how to navigate through the waters where you swim. And that is also true of life. We can all immerse ourselves in the knowledge and advice of others, but ultimately we choose our own way through the challenges we face in our lives. But it is essential to remember that in both swimming and in life we must seek help to find our way if we are unable to do so alone.

CHAPTER 7

WAX AND WANE

The surf raged through a shimmery, silver sea below a beaming moon. The wind from the previous day's storm had passed, leaving big waves breaking in a pulsing tide. I had set off at the eastern end of the beach at Castlerock, swimming out along the edge of the pier, before turning to the west. Waves and swell criss-crossed as they broke and rebounded from the wall of the pier. It was a chaotic scene among waves towering well overhead, with water feeling deep and powerful around me.

Night swimming and the moon

When I swim at night, I keep an eye on the moon. The moon gives structure to night and tide, and provides varying degrees of light. I don't rely on it as a source of light because we get so much heavy cloud cover here. However, where you live, the nights may be much clearer and you may find the light from the moon creates a more reliable source.

On the darkest nights, my eyes instinctively hunt for any fragment of light across the surface of the jet-black sea. It feels like swimming on the edge of the world and as if, at any moment, I could disappear into the abyss. When the weather cloaks the lights of distant villages to the east and the west there is little to no light on the surface of the water. But a lonely navigation light pulses at the end of the stone and concrete pier at the Barmouth, Castlerock. It feels like the light marks the edge of the world as it defiantly protrudes out through the breaking surf. Its light is both a warning and a beacon of hope on the darkest nights. Just like hypnosis, it draws my eye and focuses my swim.

In contrast to this complete darkness, if the sky is clear and the moon is in the night sky, the darkness feels less black and white. A blend of soft light and shadow create a scene that overwhelms the edge of the earth, feathering the edges of what previously felt like a place of no return. It is a reminder that, no matter what darkness we face, it is rarely completely black and white. If we keep swimming through those dark waters, over time, more light will appear and lighten the abyss we may have created in our mind.

Winter and summer

In summer, when the days are long and the nights are short, I tend not to night swim. My life is full of the world's natural light. I wake with sunrise, and I swim or surf before others wake, and I do the same late into sunset. My life is busy, exciting and full of energy as I embrace the outdoors. I live on the north coast of Ireland where, in the height of summer, the sunset dips below the horizon for only a few hours before reappearing in the east. It is a stark contrast to the dark nights in the depths of winter. In summer it can be bright until midnight and in winter the light dwindles by 4pm.

In winter I love the definite split between night and day. I tend to night swim in the months of December to the

114

end of March. In these dark, wintery nights, the presence of the moon is much more apparent than in any other season. Although the moon doesn't produce any of its own light, the light reflected off its surface by the sun increases as the relative positions of the sun and moon change.

The phases of the moon

The phases of the moon are referred to as "lunation". They represent how the moon appears to us as it moves around our planet. We generally recognize eight phases of the moon, based on a combination of cultural and scientific ideas. However, it is worth remembering that these phases are not actual events in the sky, and are, in fact, nothing more than a human interpretation of what is happening in the universe, with the transition of light and shadow. In reality, the moon orbits earth and, depending on its position, varying degrees of light from the sun is reflected across its surface giving us the view that the moon is shining in the night sky.

The eight phases are regarded as a structure for standardizing the cycle of the moon and they transition as follows:

- **New moon:** The moon aligns with the sun, and isn't illuminated. Tides are biggest.

- **Waxing crescent:** A sliver of light begins to appear.

- **First quarter:** Half-moon.

- **Waxing gibbous:** More than half-illuminated.

- **Full moon:** Moon is fully illuminated. Tides are biggest.

- **Waning gibbous:** Moon illumination shrinks from full to half moon.

- **Last quarter:** Half-moon.

- **Waning crescent:** Illumination decreases to zero.

Celts, Native Americans, Irish, Chinese and many more people have their own interpretations of the moon and what it means depending on their culture, lifestyle and beliefs. To me this seems like a relevant and natural response to understanding the moon from the perspective of the person viewing it, and their need to understand when more or less light may be available, or bigger or smaller tides may occur. This approach transcends into night swimming perfectly.

Swimming in the moonlight

It matters only to us as individuals how we perceive the moon at our own swim spot. In one area of the sea where I swim, the moon doesn't reach the water because of the towering cliffs. If I swim on a high tide, I may not be able to see the full moon unless I swim very late at night when it is higher. You may have mountains, trees or cliffs where you swim, causing an obstruction to the light from the moon.

As the moon moves through its phases, it does result in different levels of light across the cycle, as listed above. As picturesque as that may sound, it isn't always helpful for swimming. The cloud cover plays a massive part, and even a full moon may find you swimming in a much darker sea than you expected.

When the new moon phase is beginning, there is no moon in the sky. If the sky is clear, it is often black or very starry depending on cloud cover. However, there can still be some light; low white cloud can cause the lights from towns and villages to reflect off its underside and produce some light, even in the darkest of nights. Likewise, streetlights in the distance can create patches of light on the water's surface, especially if it is a calm night in the water.

So, although the moon may create light where we swim, understanding the location and the features of the landscape are crucial in understanding if any light will reach the water and if so, how much, and when. And that is true of life. We may find something that brings great light to us in dark times, but the effect of that light may be hindered or magnified by other factors in the landscape of our lives.

The moon's grip on the water

With the new moon and the full moon stages of lunation, when the earth, moon and sun are in alignment, there is greater pressure on the ocean, causing the tides to be at their highest and lowest of their cycle. With this alignment of energy forces, the power created is transferred into the atmosphere and the water. When these forces coincide with deep winter weather systems, huge swells and currents form, creating an environment in the water that requires extreme caution or complete avoidance.

These bigger tides move faster than we can swim. Do not attempt to swim against their movement.

Before you swim, take time to observe the water, read the weather and tide forecasts, and consider any other local phenomenon which might be amplified by a big tide that may also affect your swim spot. Just as the moon is in constant movement, tides are never completely static, despite humans trying to understand them in stages. Tides are usually thought of in six-hourly phases (hour one being low and six being high). Every location on the coast is different though. For example, where I swim, the tide may be high but if I was to move a few miles east the tide may have already turned. When tides move, water fills in around headlands, islands, man-made structures and rocks, and in doing so, is pushed around the coast. It doesn't move in a uniform manner "in and out". This creates currents that aren't necessarily visible or audible and in big tides this can be extremely dangerous. At times, the movement of the tide against these coastal features can be heard, but not always. I wouldn't swim in conditions where the tide is moving extremely quickly in and around rocks or structures. I'd wait, choose a different spot where the water is slack, or simply not swim.

I often find at my local swimming spot, that if the tide is low around midday, with a swell due to peak in size by the afternoon, then the next high tide that evening will amplify this swell. The waves will break with more power and size and rush further up the beach, before surging back and creating wild currents in the process.

The water at low tide has a feel like it is holding everything back, like a coiled spring ready to explode, as all the earth's energy pours into the ocean. By high tide in

118

those conditions the scene will be almost unrecognizable from earlier in the day. At other times, if no low-pressure system is present and the sea is calm, the water will still rise and fall significantly, and although it may appear tame to the untrained eye on those nights, the water is always moving, and currents lurk. Any rise and fall in water level, regardless of swell and wind, creates movement.

You can research your local swim spot using tidal charts (see Chapter 4), but this must be paired with observation over a long time to truly understand and be able to judge what the water conditions may actually be like to swim in.

Observing the moon and tides serves as a starting point for understanding the water where you swim. Like everything in life, however, conditions are constantly evolving. Through experience you can develop a real connection to your swim spot, as you become more in tune with the natural world and its moon, tides, water and light.*

---

* Understanding tidal patterns is crucial for safe swimming but keep in mind that tides can create powerful currents, especially when combined with other environmental factors like strong winds or storms. Always take time to assess local conditions and never assume you can predict the water's behaviour based solely on tides or the moon.

CHAPTER 8
OCEAN DEVOTION

The faint glow of sunrise begins to brighten the darkness of night. Rays of golden light break through the windows, pushing darkness around the room before banishing it from sight. I rise to feel the glow on my face and see the dark ocean slowly absorbing the new day's light into the shadowy surface of a fresh autumn swell. The white spray from the breaking waves reaches for the light as it drifts in the brisk, offshore breeze. The surf is alive with waves dancing their way to shore. With each wave, the tide surges and spills over undulating sand, before rushing back into the depths.

A lifetime of ocean devotion tells me that, in the next hour, the tide will likely peak and magnify into the best surf conditions of the day. I feel called to go at that moment. My wetsuit is still wet from last night's swim. I wince for a moment as I haul the soggy, sandy neoprene over me, before running barefoot across the sand. I can feel the energy of the swell rising as the tide has its final moments of push. A beautiful unbroken wave rises from the ocean, pushed from the deep water by the shallow sandbanks below. Each wave is like a page from the ocean's sacred script, a fraction of a story I read at dawn.

The offshore breeze rushes to meet the wave and throws spray into the sky, where the sunlight kisses it "Good morning". This is the moment when all the elements collide. The energy runs through my body as every muscle and fibre in me flows with this beautiful

natural element. My mind is deeply immersed in the
moment, reading and learning before the ocean turns the
page in this ancient text.

Connecting to a higher power

Some people believe in and worship deities that once existed
as people on earth. Others have a god that may represent
a force on earth or the universe. One common trait is
that, whatever is being worshipped, usually has a power
far greater than us. There is often a mystery surrounding
it, along with the power to give life, provide comfort and
to challenge our thinking. If we, as humans, can accept
that we can have a connection with a power much greater
than ourselves, then I believe that water may be the most
accessible and powerful force on earth that offers that.

The water gives lessons in many ways. We can learn
to read the water, recognize what it may be teaching
us, and take those learnings into daily life. We can be
taught about the water by other humans, but we cannot
understand the learnings the water gives to us unless we
directly create a connection to it ourselves.

Two people listening to the same piece of music are not
necessarily affected by it in the same way. One may fall in
love with the lyrics, and derive a life lesson from that, and
the other may like the way it sounds, or how it lifts their
mood. The same is true of the water. Not everyone that
spends time in and around water will acquire the same
lessons or experience.

If we, as humans, open our minds to accept the
teachings of other entities, gods or deities, then we should
also be able to recognize the power of water. I encourage

you to actively engage with your thoughts and be open to receive lessons from it.

Drawn to water

Water covers 71 per cent of the earth's surface. Humans are said to be about 60 per cent water. Water is a real, tangible force, and has an undeniable effect on everything it touches. We are drawn to water, not just for survival, but also for relaxation and renewing our energy. We often spend holidays and weekends close to the water because of the feeling of freedom it represents to us. The broad horizon is a stark contrast for many people living in built-up communities, and many of us seem to crave it. A huge amount of holiday resorts are based on the coast, and beside lakes and rivers for that reason.

Studies conducted by the University of California, Davis showed that people who viewed the water of a swimming pool had reduced heart rate and blood pressure compared to those who didn't. A second study showed that people that viewed a local waterway also had lower blood pressure and heart rate than when they viewed the ground nearby. Participants reported feeling more relaxed if the body of water was wider. We go to the water because we know it makes us feel better. Consciously, and subconsciously, we feel that pull.

Forming a connection with water can be an enriching experience, but it is essential to take practical safety measures too. The ocean can be unpredictable, and it is important to remain vigilant and well-prepared, no matter how familiar or drawn to it you may feel.

My relationship with the sea

I believe the water has its own wisdom. How that is interpreted depends on how it is received and by whom. Water can be seen to move with a blend of beauty, calmness, chaos and grace, all of which reflect how we experience life ashore.

Although I don't suggest praying to the water as a god, I do believe there are many lessons that can be taken from its power, movement and unpredictability. The lessons from the water can be used in our lives, here on the land, to help ourselves and each other make sense of humankind and the world in which we live.

When I started night swimming, I immediately recognized the similarities between the sea and life on land. The sea is unstoppable, and while swimming in it, no matter how prepared I may be, I am at its mercy. And that is true of life – life, too, is unstoppable. But if we see life as the sea and recognize that the waves and currents will not stop, then we learn to accept that, and keep swimming through life, regardless.

Ishka Jalen

My connection to the water has led to the creation of what I call the "Ishka Jalen". The name is derived from the phonetic spelling and pronunciation of the Irish words *uisce dialann*, meaning water diary. The Ishka Jalen is a body of knowledge I have built through decades of experience and is stored subconsciously. It is not a physical document or journal but an evolving, internal archive. It is composed from every swim, surf, row or walk by the water.

You might observe surfers who seem to know where to be and when. They may appear to be simply floating around as lots of waves pass by and then, by chance, they catch a wave to surf. But this isn't the case. They know exactly what they are looking for, based on a lifetime in the water. They know precisely where to be to catch a particular wave and so they wait for it to present itself. When they catch a wave, they draw from immense experience to make subtle adjustments to speed and positioning to ride the wave in the most efficient way. Experience allows them a subconscious foresight and ability to predict the future as this force of nature contorts and surges toward shore. Feelings of fear and doubt are recalled, and memories of actions and reactions taken on many other waves are drawn upon to navigate across the water's last few moments in the form of a wave. It is a beautiful thing to witness.

I first noticed people recording their experience with water at Mavericks in California in the 1990s. The big wave surfers recorded surf conditions that were over a significant height in a journal, so they were able to look back over years and establish the best conditions for that surf spot. They simply created a chart to record wave size, relative to the swell being captured on the wave buoys offshore. That concept of recording what they experience from the water stuck with me.

Unlike the physical notes that the big wave surfers created, the Ishka Jalen is a living, continually evolving, internal script, written by the water itself, based on my experience within it. Every ripple, wave, current or moment in the water is a page in the script logged in my subconscious and drawn upon as a guide every time I am in the water. This imagined scribe is an archive of feelings, emotions, actions and reactions to the water, which helps keep me safe in the water, as I adapt my knowledge to the different conditions I swim in.

Your Ishka Jalen will be your own deeply personal map, shaped by your own unique connection with the water. Fragments of knowledge, experience and memory become an evolving guide to the mystery of the water all beautifully stored within you.

Your Ishka Jalen will evolve over time. With every inter-action, observation and connection with the water, it will grow and build into pages of an elaborate internal script of knowledge so detailed, it could never be completely transcribed into written words.

Living life by the tide

If we open our minds to the potential that water is, in fact, a higher power, we invite opportunity for guidance, life lessons and a companion in dark times. If we accept the lessons offered, water can provide emotional stability, teach us about humility, patience and many other aspects of life. Followers of its teachings can incorporate mindful practices into their life that teach gratitude, resourcefulness, self-sufficiency and more. Our modern, busy lives can often feel detached from the natural world, but through some simple habits formed around the water we can reconnect to our natural world and to ourselves.

All around the coast there are people living a way of life like no other. The pull of the tide has gripped their entire beings so strongly that they have surrendered themselves to it. This isn't about adventure, the thrill of riding a wave, or the exhilaration of swimming in a raging sea . . . it's about devotion. It is a simple, mindful life lived deeply connected to the rhythm of the sea. Take only what is needed from the sea and give back when you can. This is a life rich in connection, purpose and love. A conscious attempt to lash oneself to the pulse of the ocean and cut free from the shackles that could prevent this earthly connection from thriving.

Life by water is lived in line with the seasons and the cyclical patterns of give-and-take. The changing seasons bring an abundance of opportunity for deep contemplation and devotion to the water's power and energy. Our minds can be consumed with observation and study of the sea. It's movements and the patterns it creates with every wave and surge lead to constant wonder, questioning and a never-ending desire to find the reasons behind its behaviour. This holistic way of life drowns out the noise and chaos of the modern world, returning to a more basic and, in some ways, primitive life. Focus shifts to what is really important for a life well-lived, a true connection to the world around us, its elements and the sustenance it can provide.

Living by the tide creates a wonderful appreciation of the balance in the natural world. The calm before a storm, the rain to replenish the land after days of sunshine, the raging surf of winter contrasted with the calmer weather of summer. Acceptance of the ocean's unpredictability is cultivated through years of a life lived by the tide, not by time. Knowing and accepting that the sea does not allow for swimming today and that surfing or walking is a better option, becomes second nature. Accepting that there is no driftwood for the fire in summer, and no shoals of mackerel in winter, is another example of becoming at peace with the seasonal life by the sea.

Night swimming as meditation

My discovery of night swimming as a form of meditation was a reaction to a chaotic situation the world was facing: the Covid 19 pandemic. I was struggling to accept the new norm of indefinite lockdowns, restrictions and the complete upheaval of life we all faced. I needed a way to cut out the noise and centre myself. Life felt unbalanced in this time of darkness. I decided that the dark, and this new reality, was exactly what I needed to face. So, I returned to the sea, but I did so at night.

The dark enabled me to focus on regaining my connection to the natural world I have known all my life. It allowed me the chance to remove the distractions that were clouding my peace and connect to the ocean through my senses. Like I explain in Chapter 2, the attention on how my senses and my body felt in the dark led me into a meditative state of heightened awareness and inner peace. The chaos of the world may have been mirrored in the chaos of the water, but I know the water. I understand why it appears chaotic. So, I felt more comfortable in the water than in the unpredictability of the world we were all suddenly living in.

To this day, I find the patterns and the movement of water more understandable, easier to read, and more easily explained than those of humans. Everything in the water seems balanced, flowing and required. Making sense of decisions made by other people in reaction to the situation at that time was not easy and was causing huge instability in the world.

My sense of balanced mind returned as soon as I ventured onto the beach in the dark. I didn't even need to be in the water. The dark drew my senses to the sounds of the water and the feel of the cold sand underfoot, as I walked to the water. This was the release of tension making way for the flow of the water's energy. The walk across the sand was like my body stretching and my mind calming before the full meditative experience would begin. Many others, who may previously had very little connection to the water other than on holidays, began to travel to be at the coast, lakes or rivers, and kindled a new connection to the water through dipping, swimming and paddleboarding.

Clearing the mind

Meditation is about being present with your thoughts. I found that night swimming has been both a meditative practice and a temporary release from the world. It is not possible to completely zone out in an environment that commands attention of mind, body and soul, but through that demand for attention comes a distraction-free mind where only important thoughts are left to be processed.

My night swims often involve a journey along a dark, empty beach late at night. During that walk, my mind tends to flirt between the major events of my daily life and the smaller, more insignificant happenings. I think this is an important stage in night swimming because it allows me to process thoughts and feelings before entering the water where I need to be as connected to what I am doing as possible.

While I night swim, I don't ever fully enter a "meditative state", because of the environment in which I swim. The water is often chaotic and unpredictable, so I have to keep some thoughts on my position in the water and safety, and I would advise others to do the same. So, I believe the meditative part of night swimming happens, for me, personally, before I enter the water. It is part of the process of night swimming.

You may find a different experience to mine at your swim spot, depending on how calm it is, your ability, knowledge and how at ease you are where you swim.

No matter when the meditative process takes place with night swimming, it is, without doubt, connected to the water through the senses. I find the sound of the environment to be extremely grounding and it pulls my thoughts into my mind. My focus and attention move from the external to the internal and thoughts seem more structured and less chaotic. The cold, on the other hand, is not a positive factor in the water, in my opinion. Through decades of surfing and swimming, I have only ever found the cold to be a negative distraction, prisoning my mind in the pain of ice-cold hands or feet and taking my attention away from the focus required to perform on a wave or to swim through the dark.

Lessons the water can teach you

I am fortunate that I can draw upon knowledge gained from every ocean on the planet. I have learned some valuable lessons from the sea that have guided me through some of the most troubled waters of my life:

Lesson 1: Agility in the currents of life

The push-and-pull of the sea is not showing us direction and where to swim. It is, in fact, indicating to us to find our *own* direction, despite the currents of life all around. It is teaching us to recognize windows of opportunity amidst the flows of life and be confident in our ability to pursue them. It is teaching us to be aware of the various influences in life and to investigate, evaluate, and to make our own decisions on where we are going next and why. Currents change with little warning and so we must always be agile, aware and have a dynamic approach to life. This is an important lesson to learn because so often we can feel like life is controlling *us*. By realizing that we are, in fact, in the ocean of life and exposed to its mood and seemingly abrupt changes in direction, we can be at peace with that and navigate our own way through the dark waters we may face.

Lesson 2: Calm in chaos

The storm teaches survival amid rough water. We all face rough waters in our lives, but while these conditions present potentially dangerous consequences, we are forced to hold our ground or be overwhelmed. There are times in life that, no matter how well prepared we are with back-ups, planning and safety nets, we still find ourselves in deep water. It must be remembered that there is no escape from the storm, and we have no control of it, but it will pass. We must accept and adapt to turbulent times. We must remain calm and vigilant and determined to ride out the storm. Once the storm passes, evaluate, recover and, with new experience be prepared to face whatever comes next.

Lesson 3: Perseverance

We must keep swimming. If we do not persevere against all that we face, we allow it to sweep us away. Observe the conditions and understand the forces of life you face. Read the conditions through experience, then act. Develop so many skills in the waters of life that you can effortlessly draw upon experience to swim through the dark times with confidence.

Lesson 4: Patience

Understand that conditions are not always suited to what you want to do with your life. Through experience, realize the correct time to make your next move and do not take unnecessary risks. Be patient. Life is precious. The more experience we gain, the more it becomes clear that our energy is best conserved until the optimum conditions for progress present themselves. And when that moment comes, we can act with confidence and conviction, knowing that we have learned and prepared for action, through dedication and consistency.

Lesson 5: Enough

The sea gives us enough for what we need. When it stops giving in one way, it will give in others. Being in tune to changes in the environment can lead to an appreciation for similar changes in life. Know that, as part of our life passes, the next will come, and with that, new fruits shall blossom.

Sustenance from the sea

The sea can be an abundant source of food, warmth and life. I love that living by the water allows us to eat fresh seafood and to gather firewood, seaweed and other treasures.

Seafood

There are many convenient ways to get food in the modern world and it is not always possible for us all to stop what we are doing and become hunters and gatherers, but we can increase our appreciation for the world around us by sourcing some of the food we consume.

My diet tends to revolve around fish, caught locally where possible, and eggs from my friend's hens, Daisy and Buttercup. The hens live in a spacious garden overlooking the wild North Channel.

I am pescatarian; I don't eat meat because I like animals, and I'd rather also not eat fish, but I find it difficult to consume enough protein for my active lifestyle, so I have made that choice. I was taught to fish at a very young age by my father. In fact, I was so young I can't even remember a time that I didn't know how, and where, to fish. My dad worked on trawlers as a teenager and so passing fishing on to me was natural. We have a huge variety of fish here, caught offshore in the North Channel tide by boat, and brought ashore at Greencastle. Sometimes, though, even the experienced fisherman may yield nothing. Near shore I have found it increasingly difficult to catch fish by rod and line, which may be the result of overfishing and pollution.

At present, it is legal in Ireland to have five lobster pots without requiring a licence. I share one with my friend

Leigh. We started using it because we wanted to make sure the ritual of placing it out and baiting it was something we could both fit into our lifestyle without requiring huge amounts of time. We bait it with whatever we have left over from the catch each time, and so nothing goes to waste or is killed for bait. We keep it in the shadow of the ruins of a 500-year-old castle perched on the edge of a cliff. Dunluce Castle is famous for partially collapsing into the sea during a wild storm in 1639, taking with it the kitchens, banquet hall and everyone having dinner to their death.

We tie our pot to metal rings, and it has become a great summer exercise to clamber down the cliff and check our pot for lobster and crab. The ritual of climbing the cliff each night to retrieve the pot enforces our connection to the sea. It cultivates thankfulness for what it provides and gives Leigh and I another purpose within our friendship.

I first learned of eating limpets on a surf trip to Madeira. Locals would clamber along the black boulders below the towering cliffs and collect bags of limpets for home and the restaurants. Limpets may not be as well known as mussels as a form of food, but they are wonderfully easy to cook and eat. They aren't filter feeders like mussels, so can be a safer form of shellfish to eat as they don't accumulate toxins and bacteria as readily. Collecting limpets is a way of getting involved in harvesting your own food from the environment in which you swim, without the need for lots of time and equipment, like many other forms of fishing may require.

I often collect limpets along the rocks and cook them at home. Cook in a pan with their shells in some garlic and butter, for a freshly sourced, sustainable dish, straight from the waters where you swim.

Sea plants

Gathering seaweed, or other sea plants, is a great way to become more in tune with the spot you choose to swim. We have dandelions in our sand dunes here, and I used to collect them and make huge pots of tea with them. We also have some wild rose bushes in the dunes, with rosehips. There may be other plants or sources of nutrition at your swim spot that you are not yet aware of, such as samphire, and you could incorporate them into your daily life.

I remember sitting in the summer sunshine outside my van, in a remote part of Ireland. I noticed a man appear close to shore on the low tide. He waved up at me as he hopped from one big grey boulder to the next along the water's edge. Soon he disappeared from view and from my thoughts. I continued to sit in the summer sunshine and rare low wind when suddenly he appeared holding a fistful of dried seaweed. In a thick, country accent and a cheekful of seaweed he proclaimed, "it's the Irish chewing gum". We both chuckled and he handed me a leathery, crunchy bunch of freshly dried dulse, before he headed back off into the distance.

We have a long tradition here of using seaweed in a variety of ways. When I was a kid, in summer the local shops would sell little white paper bags filled with dulse. The salty, chewy texture of the seaweed wasn't everyone's idea of a treat, but I always looked forward to it in summer. There are lots of varieties of seaweed around the shores of the UK, but the main one we eat at Castlerock is dulse. It is a flat-shaped weed found in big beds underwater, or along the edge of rocks at sea level. When swells rise and fall, it can often be seen moving with the water. We also have Irish wrack, which is a bit

135

more leaf-like in appearance. It is only legal where I live to collect seaweed that is adrift. Some parts of the world may not have any restrictions on collecting it, but here it is heavily protected.

I have a cast-iron bath in my garden, below rose bushes and honeysuckle. A few lengths of dulse or wrack is an amazing addition to a hot, outdoor bath any time of year. The oils from the seaweed make the skin soft and supple. The National Library of Medicine in the USA states that seaweed has anti-aging benefits, among many other positive effects on our skin.

At the spot I collect seaweed, I only ever see one other person collecting it. He doesn't use it in his bath, but he spreads it over his vegetable garden. Seaweed can be placed over the soil beneath the trees, and as it breaks down, it leaches nutrition into the soil. *

Gathering firewood

I often walk the shore pulling an old, brown, plastic, sun-faded fishing box behind me with a piece of faded blue rope attached to it. These boxes are often discarded from fishing boats and wash up on the beach. I use them for driftwood collection and carrying my tools around in. As I walk the shore dragging the box I lift pieces of wood and drop them as I go. The challenge is making sure my dog has a stick and doesn't poach them from the box as

---

* When foraging for seafood or seaweed, always be aware of local regulations, potential pollution, and the quality of the water. Only harvest from clean, uncontaminated areas, and avoid eating shellfish or other organisms that may carry toxins or pollutants, particularly after heavy rainfall. Speak to local experts if in doubt.

I walk. This exercise is another way of connecting to the give-and-take of the water at my swim spot.

The water provides warmth through fuel for the fire all year round, and the ritual of collection, drying out and burning is deeply satisfying. The contrast between the often smaller pieces of driftwood left by the tide in summer, to the trees and logs that drift ashore in winter, creates an obvious cycle for collecting fuel for the fire. There are some little nooks and crannies on the beach that face south, and the sun bleaches the wood white and dries it out ready for the fire. Other pieces need time in the garage to dry out. It is a great feeling to sit down next to the fireplace and pull out pieces of driftwood with remnants of seaweed caught in the splits, and sand falling out of the rounded-off edges from the sea-sculpted wood.

Bringing the sea into your home

The sea is outside, but I have very much brought it indoors with me. Its gifts decorate my home, and the floor is often strewn with sand from beach walks or swims. If I see anything along the tide line that looks particularly interesting, I bring it back and place it in an old printer's drawer I have mounted on my living room wall overlooking the sea. It now houses a collection of colourful little shells, pieces of broken pottery with ornate blue and white patterns, and even a little Lego man I found on the beach that looked like he should be brought up to the house. Over the years I've found all sorts of things discarded by humans that became gifts from the sea. My mantelpiece is a large chunk of wood I salvaged from the tide right in front of my house. I dried it out and adjusted it to fit above the fire. All along it sit sea urchin shells and unusual little pieces of driftwood. Hanging over the fireplace is the skull of a goat with large, upright horns, which was mounted and presented to me by Marcus, from the Scottish island of Islay. He had found the animal directly above the place where I made it ashore after the first-ever crossing between Ireland and Islay by paddleboard. On a clear day I can see the spot from my living room window, next to where the skull now hangs as a reminder.

Broken lobster pots become plant pots, old rope becomes a tow rope, and floats and buoys become decorations in the garden. This is a beautiful way to keep close to the sea, to collect memories, and to constantly remind myself of the sea and the passing of time.

Beach cleaning

"In Japanese Buddhism, it is said that what you must do in the pursuit of your spirituality is clean, clean, clean. This is because the practice of cleaning is powerful."

Shoukei Matsumoto

Unfortunately, there is a huge pollution issue in many parts of the world, with a lack of respect for the sea, and so beach cleaning has become necessary. I prefer the approach of prevention is better than cure, but when you enjoy the environment as much as I do, you will find it difficult to ignore litter that has been dropped on the beach, or leave something that has been washed ashore for the tide to collect again later.

Locals to the beach tend to care so much that we often pick up litter we didn't drop, such as plastic, glass and even discarded nappies. I know people who take an annual trip out to the mouth of Lough Foyle in Co. Derry to clean up the plastic and rubbish which accumulates in the corner of a sandy cove right next to where the lough flows into the sea. I know others who wade through the shallows of Lough Neagh, Britain's largest lake, and collect plastic waste caught in the reeds.

"The 2 Minute Beach Clean" is a great initiative by Martin Dorey, in that he managed to place beach cleaning stations around the country to help tackle beach pollution. There are now over 1,000 around the UK, encouraging people to take their rubbish home, and to clear it up when they see it. Always take care when beach cleaning, especially when handling hazardous materials. Consider wearing gloves and using a litter picker.

Many surfers and swimmers have a ritual where they will pick up a piece of rubbish every time they visit the beach, as a way of giving back to the sea.

Cleaning the beach, or the location where we swim, can have an even deeper impact on us than the simple act of picking up litter. The ritual of removing litter creates satisfaction for us, and returns the area to its natural state, creating a more harmonious environment. This then contributes to us having a clearer and cleaner mind for swimming, relaxing and meditation.

To show your love of the water, we could all take inspiration from #Take3fortheSea:

- Take three pieces of rubbish with you when you leave the beach, waterway . . . or anywhere.

- Take three actions to reduce your consumption of single-use plastic.

- Take three people on the journey with you.

Night swimming can be at the heart of our connection with the environment. Guidance flows into daily life, giving us moments of reflection and gratitude for the life we have chosen with the water.

CHAPTER 9
BOWING TO THE WATER

Dark, inky water gently crept ashore, crossing the reflection of the moon on the ripples of wet sand. The water's energy slowed as it rose up the beach, before momentarily stopping in front of my feet. The night was still and cold clung to my bare hands as I soaked in the magical winter moonlight. The wild North Atlantic was, for once, lying almost perfectly still, other than the gentle pulse of energy moving in the night. As it paused before its next breath, I too paused, bowing my head in a quiet moment of respect.

A moment of respect

The bow to the water is the portal through which I transition from the noise of life to the quiet tranquility of the water. I let go of life's demands, offload the weight I'd carried to the shore, and enter a state of focus tied to the rhythm of the sea. I exhale in time with the water as it begins to draw back into itself, pulling the water and me with it. With my mind and body now present and connected to the water, I walk with its breath, stepping into the water until I start swimming.

Much like in martial arts, where the bow symbolizes respect, here before the sea, it also serves as a moment of centring and focus. It grounds me, pulling my mind and body into alignment with the sea. I believe, if you adopt this ritual, you too can deepen your experience with the water where you swim, and use it to help you find clarity in your life.

The origins of my bow

In 1990, my parents took me to watch a karate class. In a quiet corridor on the first floor of the local leisure centre, I watched through the window as a stream of children stepped into the room. One by one, the children paused for a moment, placed their feet together, hands by their sides and dipped their head slightly, appearing to bow into the room. I wondered why they were bowing and what it meant. The beige, carpeted room, the practice and the bow all seemed "quieter" than I had imagined, and not like I'd seen in the films! The following week I joined the class. Like everyone else did, I bowed as I entered the room. I still didn't know why I was bowing, but it felt significant.

I later learned that bowing was not about submitting to someone or something. It was not about a higher power, or someone being perceived as of more significance than another. It is simply about respect – respect for the space where training is taking place and acknowledgement of the hard work the Sensei had put into making the space the home of the martial art. And respect of the traditions around the art, the history and culture that students were entrusted to carry on.

Something about this practice seemed so natural and ingrained in me that I subconsciously took the principle of bowing from karate to the sea. Intuitively, I

142

had begun to blend the teachings from one area of life, into that of another, recognizing the need for respect in all that we do.

Just like martial arts, the water, too, is a space, a teacher and a tradition that commands respect. My ritual of bowing to the sea is no different to that of martial arts. I simply walk to the edge of the water and, before the water's touch, I pause for a moment, look to the horizon and bow. I do the same when I exit the water. It is so subtle no one would even notice it happening. It is not a grand gesture or an obvious movement, but to me it represents a respect for the environment I am a part of.

Different things go through my mind at that moment of the bow. Sometimes my mind is already focused on the water, the surf and the swim conditions and I'm excited to get out there. Sometimes, though, heavier things enter my mind, like family and friends that are no longer with us. Sometimes, with so much history and lore where I live, for a second, I might imagine old boats passing by, or what life might be like on a tanker I can see lit up out at sea.

The bow can have different meanings and depths for each one of us. For me, the following four thoughts form the basis of my reasons for bowing to the water. Perhaps some will resonate with you:

Honouring those lost at sea
The sea has taken the lives of many souls. In Ireland it is said that the souls of lost fishermen and sailors become seagulls. The area where I swim is surrounded by the squawking and swooping of gulls that nest in the cliffs, watching over the waters as I swim. A reminder that the water takes life. The water holds the bodies of those

lost, becoming part of the water and therefore part of the energy of the water in which we swim. To swim in the water is to immerse ourselves in the lives that it took and held on to. It is to bathe in the history, the passion, love, courage and belief of all those that ventured across the water and never returned. By swimming in the sea, we carry on their tradition and connection to the water and honour their spirit. Through honouring the lost, we remind ourselves to be cautious and mindful of the dangers of the water and how vulnerable we can be in the face of its power.

Humility

Acknowledging the water as a power much greater than us, and being grateful that I can enjoy it. The moment of the bow is time to pause and remember that, despite many years of experience, the water can take us in an instant. Water has depths and mystery we will never completely understand, and therefore a pause and bow are acknowledgement of that. A time to remember our place in the environment and of our vulnerability.

Reverence for those that came before

We are specks in the ocean of the generations the water has witnessed come and go. Many things we know about how to live, and survive, in and around the water, have been passed down by those populations, over time. We carry that knowledge and spirit for now, but at some point, we will also become someone "that came before". We must live with the respect that we are not the first, nor the last, but are part of a current flowing through the waters of life. Many people passed through here before us and many more will pass after us. Remembering this through a moments pause and bow is a reminder of where we come from, and where we are going.

Thanks Giving

Acknowledging the gift of the water for the life it gives to us. Being thankful for the nourishment of life as the water flows through every cell in our body and mind, allowing us many different connections to the water. A pause and bow to the water to acknowledge the depths it has reached within us, bringing us to life, with waves of energy that pass from us and into the world.

Creating your own bow

A bow before you swim can be personal to you. Bowing can introduce a new dimension and layer of meaning into your experience with the water, so choose what feels meaningful to you. Before you allow the emotional connection to wash over you, remember that safety is your primary responsibility. The water may be a source of comfort, but it is also a force that must be respected. For me, a bow remains rooted in respect, but it doesn't need to be. The act itself is a simple gesture, one that can be personalized to suit your unique connection to the water where you swim. If you are new to swimming, or it is primarily a fitness endeavour, introducing a bow to your routine can bring a profound new depth:

Finding personal meaning

Have you ever asked yourself if you have a deeper connection to swimming, or night swimming, than you maybe once thought? Many people see the water as a form of escape, something they do with a social circle, to be in nature, or maybe even to deal with pain. It may be a simple hobby at the outset. But I believe that, over time, our connection to the water deepens. Without realizing, we start to build an emotional connection to it. You may be thankful and grateful for having the water in your life, like I am, and a simple moment to pause and bow to acknowledge that, before and after every swim, might be more than enough. A bow nurtures mindfulness of how fortunate we are to have the ability and freedom to be in the water. You may also consider nature and remind yourself how swimming has brought you closer to the natural world.

A moment of reflection

During the physical pause and bow is a good time to reflect on life. Memories and experiences in life may cross your mind and heart, offering you a newly found moment for personal reflection. A brief time to reflect and then move on. This reflective moment can allow you a fresh perspective on the struggles of daily life before leaving them behind as you enter the water. When night swimming, we have a choice: we can either accept the minimal light that is reflected back to us from the surface of the water, or we can become lost in the overwhelming darkness. By allowing the sources of light that reflect in the water to guide us through our swim, we inherently seek the light, despite the vast amount of darkness that surrounds it, allowing us to swim with a sense of direction and purpose.

The same principle is true of life. Many people are living through extremely dark times: the pressures of daily life, financial problems, relationship issues and lots of other heavy life experiences. That darkness can overwhelm us, and if we let it, its reflection may be all that we see in our lives, reminding us of the difficulties we face. But, like in the water, we must look for the glimmers of light, the little moments that light our path. Through focusing on those positives, brighter light will be reflected into our lives, overcoming the darkness.

So, in the moment of your bow allow that pause and take a moment to reflect on the light in your life, rather than the darkness. This could create another moment in your day where you slow down, take stock of life, become present, and at the same time acknowledge and respect the water for the wonderful light it brings to your life.

As part of your life journey

Just like the water itself, the meaning and experience of the bow may change as you journey through life and through the water. The bow may symbolize something particular to you today, but as you flow with the current of life, the symbolization may evolve with you on your journey. Recognizing those changes in a momentary pause is a mindful way of being aware of where we are in our unique journey.

Respect for history

When you think of your swim spot, what do you know? Do you know the history of where you swim? Have you learned about the water, what it was used for long before you decided to swim there, or considered who may have crossed it or even created it? For example, many large rock pools have been created by humans by damming off the water to provide space for safe, recreational swimming. Some rivers are ancient routes or have been the battle lines of previous conflict.

147

Every body of water has a history that we become part of, and acknowledging it can bring a new layer of depth and meaning to why we are swimming there.

The waters at my swim spot have a history of: Viking landings; a Spanish Armada boat sinking; World War vessels and arms dumped at sea; Irish sea lords and trade; as well as being where people fled to America in the hope of a better life. All this rich history fills the water with a unique atmosphere that I am thankful to swim in.

By bowing to the sea when I swim, it is a simple gesture of respect to all those happenings, to the loss of life, and futures crafted on the sea. Take time and learn about your waters, and draw that knowledge into your own moment of pause and respect before you enter and leave the sacred waters you have become so attached to.

A customized movement

The bow doesn't need to look a certain way. Some martial artists believe in a deep breath and a very pronounced bow, some people are content with a discreet nod. Personally, I lean more toward a discreet nod to the horizon, that I blend effortlessly into my preparation before entering the water. I would not want to draw attention to myself and so I prefer to be low-key about it, but it can be whatever you want it to be. You could incorporate words, maybe a mantra you live by that you say out loud or inward to yourself. It could incorporate religious gestures such as crossing yourself. It could be something you share with other people, or do alone. When I first went to surf in California, one of the big wave surfers gathered three of us in a circle on the sand. He asked us to close our eyes, and he said a few words. Although not strictly a bow, the principal was the same.

The key is that the bow should be a moment in your day and your swim preparation to stop, offer respect, gather your thoughts and to mark your crossing of the threshold between land and the water.

The deepest bow

Three days after the sudden passing of my father, I finally mustered the strength to pull myself away from the devastation and drive my brother and myself to the beach to surf. In one way, it felt completely selfish and unnecessary to even contemplate going to surf amid such a traumatic life event. But this return to the water was not about the joy of riding waves, it was about something much deeper. We had both been introduced to the water by our dad and it has been the focal point of both our lives. I felt by going there, it was a way to reconnect with him.

We hadn't arranged to meet anyone there, it was just us going surfing, but coincidentally we met friends who were also going into the water. They offered their condolences, and for the first time, I was faced with the reality of Dad's passing, through the words of others. The shock of hearing them acknowledge the loss of him hit me hard. It suddenly felt even more real.

I walked down the path to the shoreline, my head hung low. I was in no fit state of mind to be throwing myself into pumping surf, but I knew I needed to.

I paused for a moment to look out to the horizon. Over a decade after starting the ritual of bowing to the sea, I closed my eyes and bowed my head. The moment brought a wave of emotion, taking me from the land, which my father had left, to the water, where I felt he was. My dad was a swimmer. He would stand on the pier at Castlerock leaning against the pole halfway along it, watching me surf or swim, and filming me as I rode the waves. He was always with me in the sea.

For the first time in my life, my bow to the water took me into a new dimension. Not many waves were ridden that day, but I drove home feeling better for the experience. It became a tradition for me when surfing in Castlerock to bow to the water, but also to bow to the place on the pier where Dad stood for all the years that he watched and helped me learn to surf.

The moment of pause and respect that had been a ritual to me changed with that life event. As my journey continues, so, too, do the depths and layers of gratitude, honour, respect and thanks that are embedded in my bow to the water.

I urge you to look deep into your own life, reflecting on the significant experiences that make you who you are. Find connection to those around you, to places, memories and good times. Draw them into your presence and recognize the importance they played in building you into the person you are. See them clearly, and in your quiet moment before and after swimming you can acknowledge them, pay respect to them, and honour them for their significance in your life. It is through quiet moments of reflection that we find true understanding and self-awareness of ourselves, allowing clarity as we swim through the darkest times of life.

CHAPTER 10

THE STORM

Thrashes of wind tear into the surface of a raging, dark sea, driving the water into mountainous peaks and troughs before collapsing and surging all around me. A frothy white surface lights the way, before the next avalanche of white water thrusts from the dark night and rushes overhead. Its thump shudders through me before I am dragged, then released, for a gasp of salty, cold air. I break into my swim stroke, flowing with the torrent crafted by the storm.

Swimming through the darkest storms

It was just four days before Christmas, and I still hadn't put a tree up. The tree lay on its side behind the sofa, but my mind had been too distracted in recent days to put it up. A mixture of excitement and anticipation flowed through me for days as the storm intensified. An apocalyptic forecast of 112 kmph (70-mph) westerly winds and a 6-metre (30-feet) swell converged to form the biggest storm of winter. News reports filled the media channels with warnings to stay indoors and avoid coastal areas because of large storm surges. Storm Pia was brewing in the North Atlantic, mid-December 2023. The storm looked likely to coincide with the winter solstice on the night of the 21st – the shortest day and longest night of the year.

It is the moment before the earth turns back toward the sun and new light begins to enter our world. I felt compelled to swim in this symbolic moment in time.

If night swimming has taught me anything about life, it is that I must swim through the darkest of storms to emerge stronger. To face the unknown through dedication to finding the light in dark times. To choose to not swim through this storm would be disloyal to myself and to the environment that has taught me resilience, perseverance and dedication.

I planned to swim my biggest distance to date. I would not let these conditions overpower me; instead, I would calculate how to use them to my advantage. I hoped to inspire anyone that was following my Swim Through Darkness Campaign, and facing the darkest and worst conditions in their life, to stay strong. I hoped to inspire people to look at what they faced in their internal storms in life and use that experience and knowledge to keep going through the biggest storms in the darkest nights. Swimming in extreme weather conditions, such as storms with high winds and large swells, is incredibly dangerous and should not be attempted. I am only able to swim in these conditions at my swim spot through a series of carefully calculated plans based on a lifetime spent in this particular location. I do not recommend anyone attempt swimming in such conditions.

Making a plan

I calculated carefully where, and when, to swim; I was quietly confident that the conditions would produce the perfect set-up for swimming a big distance in the surf zone after dark. The peak of the storm's energy looked like it would coincide with the tide dropping off high to around mid-tide at my swim spot. I believed that the water flow would probably match the direction of the wind and the monstrous swell at sea.

The current would find its way through the gulleys between the sandbanks more easily than at any other stage of tide. The water at low tide tends to flow with a more defined direction than it does at a higher tide. On the higher tide, the water often floods the gulleys between the sandbanks which makes the water sloshier and more erratic as it struggles to get back out to sea through the surf. The lower tide, in the forecast sea conditions, would most likely produce a conveyor belt-type flow along large sections of the beach. With all these factors lined up, it was a fairly safe bet to make that swimming west to east would be the way to take advantage of the conditions.

Despite my planning, I always have a little butterfly in the pit of my stomach when the weather charts are that extreme. I constantly check the weather forecasts and wave buoys right up until I enter the water. I look at several sources for information, but I base as much as possible on visually checking the coast, several times a day, in the lead up to this kind of a storm. I had been swimming every night in December in progressively wilder conditions. The previous chaotic seas were a warm-up.

Please note: It is important to build an understanding of the data you are using to make decisions around where and when to swim as there are often differences between forecasting sources and what is actually happening in real time in the water. Not every location will have a precise set of weather and water predictions and it is vital to remember that they are simply that . . . predictions.

Just like the knowledge and experience I impart, nothing can guarantee what will happen in the water and so building your own individual knowledge, based through observing the water, is crucial to swimming safely.

Huge amounts of energy would be electrifying the atmosphere and the water. It was exciting! By the time I would enter the water, the huge, open ocean swell would be making landfall. The tide would be running with the wind direction and the entire ocean would feel like it was surging to the east. My plan was to get upstream of the flow as far as safely possible and then swim with it. I expected the conditions would be so favourable that I wouldn't need to swim much anyway – I'd go with the flow and enjoy the moment. It was setting up to be an amazing night.

Reaching for help

But, like life itself, given the conditions, I felt it was sensible to call upon some friends for support. I shouldn't be facing the darkest night of winter alone, and nor should you in anything in your life. I called three friends I trusted to have my back, and told them my plans. They all committed to be on the beach that night. I often feel a hint of guilt reaching out for help; I would much rather slip out into the wild weather alone and not bother anyone, but I know they would be annoyed at me.

I need to also consider my friends' safety; if something were to happen and I needed help, it would be dangerous for anyone to enter the water. That responsibility keeps me close to shore to keep risk to a minimum.

I had a few doubts niggling in my mind, but it is perfectly normal to be apprehensive in the face of the unknown. One of my biggest concerns is being hit by something in the water. These violent storms can rip tree trunks from deep in the sea and throw them ashore. Fishing nets and even dead farm animals are not uncommon in the tide during this kind of a storm. None of these things are anything I can control, and it is highly unlikely, but still my mind tries to find something to stop me, despite my extremely calculated approach.

The day of the swim

I rose at dawn to peer out into the wild North Atlantic. At 7.30 am the light was starting to break the night into the shortest day of the year. The grey, overcast horizon began to brighten but no sun was visible in the east. Heavy cloud and rain had moved in overnight.

I wanted to see and feel the weather, so I pulled the door open. The wind slipped by me, billowing the linen curtain into the room. I stepped barefoot and topless into the grim morning. A deep, cold breath drew my shoulders to my ears, and the wind licked salt and sea-spray to form goosebumps on my skin. Blyton, my big dog, followed me out, looking much more comfortable than me. His long coat blew in the wind as he pointed his nose in the air, enjoying the moment. I stood stiff, shivering, whilst gazing ahead. There was a threatening feel in the air, like the ocean was a creature stirring, waiting and gathering its power.

I stood outside at that exact moment because I knew the tide would be at a similar stage in 12 hours' time, when I planned to swim. Seeing it now would give me some indication of what it would look like later when all the other elements would arrive.

Keeping a daily routine

Blyton and I went back indoors and had breakfast. My breakfast consists of coffee, milk and oats and a concoction of herbs, oil and fish. Blyton always sits beside me and gets his share. The simple daily ritual of pouring coffee and eating breakfast seemed like a stark contrast to the stormy sea just out the window. But the mundanity of daily life is the structure that keeps us all grounded and on track. It cannot be neglected in the face of a storm. It is vital to keep doing the things that create balance and structure in daily life if we are to face the storms with confidence and strength. We never know how long each storm will last. We don't know what exactly we will face, and how deep we will have to dig to survive it. For that reason, we need to be prepared and fit to endure whatever comes our way. There may be no time for recovery before the next storm, and so maintaining a solid structure in life, which for me includes caring for my health and multiple interests, helps with balance.

The calm before the storm

Knowing that my mind would love nothing more than to obsess all day over the approaching storm, I decided to force myself to put the Christmas tree up. The distraction as I untangled the lights and decorated the tree kept my focus off the unease I was feeling about swimming in the storm.

At 4pm, as the last glimmer of light vanished toward the winter solstice, I had my last look at the sea. I walked the dusky shoreline as massive surges of froth-filled brine powered across the sand toward me, before being dragged back into the churning surf.

Darkness descended, concealing the lonely sea's wild unrest. The howls of the wind and the roars of the sea were the only clues to the turmoil below the cover of night. I walked home, reluctant to take my eyes off the unsettled sea as it roared into the night, but I also knew that I needed to let it go, accept that I have done as much as I can, release my grip and trust.

Overcoming the darkness

I find fire mesmerizing. Each night before I swim, I light a fire. I light it outside using both driftwood and turf. It is a symbolic ritual to me and represents overcoming the impossible.

When you build a fire outdoors, the first thing you will notice is how difficult it is to light. The wind, sea-spray and cold all seem to conspire to extinguish the match sparks. It takes several strikes to overcome the elements and to position the fire so that it can light and grow. If the fire can overcome all darkness, then I believe you, too, can overcome whatever you may face in life.

I light a fire in a little clay chimenea outside my door, or at the beach, depending on where I'm swimming. On calmer nights I can even smell the smoke from the fire drifting out into the surf in the dark, serving as another little reminder that nature is guiding me as I swim through the darkness. When I return from my swim, the fire is often still lit or smouldering, fighting the darkness. We must see our mind as the spark that ignites the fire within us. We have the power to light the kindling and create a glow that overcomes all darkness, and to share that flame with others who may be struggling to light their own fire within.

We must fuel the fire within through good thoughts, exercise, nutritious food, education, sleep and life well-lived. Gather the fuel you need to feed your fire within, light your way and then help those around you ignite theirs. We must keep the fire fuelled or it will plunge us back into the dark once again.

Into the unknown

No matter how many times I night swim, I am reminded by the elements that each time is a step into the unknown. It is a wonderful way to train myself to continually go into life in search of new experiences and adventures. On this night I needed to go a few miles to the west to get upstream of the raging storm. I was clad head-to-toe in my unintentionally festive red neoprene battle suit as I drove out of the village at 6 pm. Last-minute Christmas shoppers were returning home and second-glancing me as I drove through the streets on my way to swim.

On the final approach to the beach, the road goes down a long, steep hill, passing between a forest to the south and a castle to the north. The bars on my car roof whistled and vibrated as the wind and rain was funnelled through the gap. The storm was in full flow. Many thoughts ran through my mind as I left the streetlights behind and drove onto the hard, compacted sand. Moments later, a convoy of cars drove onto the beach, their headlights beaming out into the dark, searching for me. My friends couldn't see me, but they knew I was there, somewhere. When their lights caught the white side of my car they pulled alongside. We drove together to the halfway point of the swim route and parked up in the sand dunes for some protection from the storm.

The energy in the atmosphere was immense. The plan was that the team would drive along, tracking me, in my car, rather than walk along the beach, as the weather was so bad. Once we had everything organized we drove further west to the start point and did a radio check. It was time. I bowed to the water and began to wade into the shallow flow of the river as it made its final rush for the sea.

I'm always wary of rivers entering the sea, as even seemingly gentle flows may be stubbornly running the opposite direction to the main flow underwater. I brace myself, digging my feet into the hard sand below, to steady myself against each wave as I waded further out. I was aware that, in any moment, the river could take me off my feet.

The wind was howling, with momentary pauses in its strength, as if recoiling ready for another attack. I knew the sound of the shallows would change soon, to the rush of the waves coming ashore.

This is a strange moment in the process of night swimming. The contrast between the shadowy expanse of sand on the higher beach, and the molten, inky tumult of the sea, is seamed by a shiny, hard and flatter strip of sand where the waves charge, then retreat. There is a "no-man's land" feel about this section of the beach.

Neither the sea, nor the land, lay claim to it, but they fight for it, nonetheless. At that moment I feel exposed and vulnerable, no longer embraced by shadows below the cliffs, but I haven't yet made it to the fully immersive darkness of the sea.

Ahead, the horizon was black, broken only by the waves of wild white horses galloping from the dark ocean toward the golden fields of sand behind me. They charged into me and through me as if I was so small in the vastness of the scene that they didn't even realize I was there. I was pushed and shoved until I eventually succumbed to their charge. I lay down in the mist of spray, surrendering to the wild sea. I began swimming.

On the darkest and longest night, the sea was lonely no more. I swam with it, allowing it to carry me. Like a wild animal, it thrashed, reminding me of my place in this almighty realm. With each wave it hurled, I was sent spiralling into the cauldron. I was hit so hard at one point that the radio was ripped from my hand. I panicked for a moment, because I knew my friends wouldn't be able to check on me. Underwater, I reached into the blackness, frantically grabbing out in the hope that it might be nearby, but the radio was gone. The next wave crashed behind and I threw myself into its path, allowing it to push me with it. I bodysurfed with the wave, my energy finally matching that of the ocean. Suddenly, I felt accepted in its wild tantrum. I rode the wave until by chance my hands hit the floating radio! I grabbed it, surfaced, and immediately radioed to tell them what happened. Unfazed and without delay, David replied calmly, "Carry on."

Stroke after stroke I swam with the elements as continual waves trampled overhead. Everything was exactly as I imagined it would be. The uncertainty and unease about what the darkness held for me tonight was drowned by the sea. Before long, I was in flow, moving effortlessly with the ocean current through whatever waves came from the dark.

I swam almost effortlessly through pounding surf, wave after wave, stroke after stroke. The current ploughed through a rip current, allowing me to swim a little further than planned.

The experience was so amazing that, when I finished my swim, I ran back to the start point and swam again. I racked up over 4 kilometres (2½ miles) of swimming in less than an hour. But each swim was different. Throughout that hour, the water changed; at times the flow was stronger, letting me swim further with it. It was a magical experience in the wildest and darkest of nights.

Every time I enter the sea in the dark is another new chance to overcome. It is a new chance to remind myself that I, too, am an ocean of power. I have since found myself longing for another magical night like that one. I regularly look at weather charts and hope for the wind to move and the swell to rise to produce similar conditions. It felt like it was where I was meant to be. When I was in the water, going with the flow, I felt at ease.

The energy of the wild night had adrenalized my spirit.

Returning to the fire

I returned home. The waves continued to roar, and the wind still howled as the water in my suit ran to my feet and back down the beach. I stood next to the fire. The flame was hungry for fuel, its weak glow struggling to keep going among the charred remains of driftwood and turf. It had held its own throughout the darkness while I swam, but upon my return it needed to be re-stoked. I fed it more fuel to keep it going through this dark and wild night, until the change of seasons would arrive at dawn.

Although the darkest night was passing and the storm was calming, I felt it was important to keep the fire going. The fire fought through the worst, and it must be rekindled and allowed to thrive through easier, more favourable times.

Your fire must be allowed to roar and crackle and spread light and warmth, not just for one bad night, but into every day and every night of your life. You must continue to feed your inner fire with the fuel it needs to burn brightly, and ignite the path in front of you. Now that you have it lit, do not let it go out. Through perseverance, you will never be in a place in life where you need to rebuild and ignite the flame once more. Keep it lit, be aware of the ever-changing intensity of the flame, and know when, and how, to add fuel so that you are never left in the darkness alone, ever again.

CHAPTER 11
GATHERING

Up on stage, the CEO of the International Surfing Association poured jars of sand into a large, see-through box. All colours and textures of sand, from golden to black, and fine to coarse, were added. The sand was from the coastlines where each surfer competing in the World Surfing Games honed their skills. Our Irish sand was added to the mix. In that moment, each beach, team and nation were mixed into one vessel; a symbol of unity among people who, if not for the sea, would likely remain strangers.

Mixing of the sands

This ritual has stayed with me through life, a quiet reminder that we are all part of something that doesn't recognize borders, the colour of our skin or our beliefs. Each grain of sand connects us in a way that only nature can – one ocean, one world, one community.

I have since seen the ceremony in other countries, as I represented Ireland at other events. Each time I've seen it, its significance became more apparent to me. It is a great way to symbolize inclusivity, togetherness and acceptance of each and every one of us with a connection to the water. Neither the water nor the sand discriminate. It does not matter where we are from, how we look, or what we believe – the water is a great leveller. Whether we are surfers riding the waves, walkers observing the water from the shore, or swimmers dipping in the sea – the water is for everyone.

Matilda

In the 1980s, when I learned to swim and surf in the Atlantic, it was extremely unusual to be in the sea except in summer. If someone was in the sea in the middle of winter, they were probably doing it for a dare or slightly unhinged . . . or so it would probably have been perceived.

However, at Castlerock, there was one person doing things differently. Matilda would walk the beach barefoot every day, before dipping into the wild, white surf. She was mostly alone or with one other friend. Matilda seemed almost mythical as her lonely figure headed into the sea, whatever the weather. She didn't have an expensive changing robe, a swim float or any other product that many of us outdoor swimmers see as essential kit today. She wore her swimsuit and that was it. Onlookers from the village houses no doubt noticed her as they sat indoors, wondering why on earth she would be doing such a thing on a cold winter's day.

Swimmers like Matilda didn't have access to online videos or books about outdoor swimming, teaching them about the water. They learned everything through experience, and in doing so, learned how to swim safely in the wild, embodying a relationship with the water despite it being an extremely unusual thing to do at the time.

A solitary, daily swim reflects an independent, personal relationship with the water. This is a gentle reminder that it is ok to not be part of the crowd.

Seeking connection

Many years later, Matilda's once solitary and unusual ritual, has become not just accepted by society, but celebrated, with new groups of people coming to the water. The life-altering Covid 19 pandemic brought a realization to many of how we may have taken freedom in the outdoors for granted. Being told to remain indoors led to social isolation and frustration as we recognized our need for nature more than ever. When daily exercise and travel to do so were permitted, a gold rush took place! The coasts, and other beauty spots, were awash with a tide of visitors. People travelled for miles for their socially distant exercise.

Soon, huge numbers of people were taking to cold-water dipping. Most probably inspired by the likes of Wim Hof, on one level, but maybe locally by their own Matilda, or the idea of being just like her.

As the newcomers to the water found their sea legs, they brought concern to seasoned locals. Some appeared to have very little water experience, which led to lots of rescues of paddleboarders and dippers. Before you go into the water, be sure to learn about the many factors that influence the water where you plan to swim, as we have covered in this book. Know how they may affect you and you will have a much more enjoyable and safer experience in the water.

Many coastal beaches, lakes and rivers are busier in summer as people make the most of the longer days and spend time outdoors near the water. Traditionally, where I live, we would see a distinct break in September as schools start back, and people leave the idea of being outdoors near water behind until the next season.

The families huddled behind windbreakers with BBQs lit and ice cream vans made way for the blowy white sand of ever-increasing westerly winds and large seas. The light air of holiday vibes drifted off, making way for the harsher, wilder air of autumn and winter.

But since the pandemic, we spend more time outdoors. The idea of a summer season is not so clear cut now. The autumn and winter months now attract large numbers of water lovers, too. A new-found appreciation for the outdoors blossomed and many people have nurtured that new connection ever since. Little communities of swimmers have grown into groups of friends, just as groups of friends have grown into communities of swimmers.

A new social hub has been born around the water. Dippers now meet at all hours of the day, go into the water and often congregate for a hot drink from a flask at the water's edge. The dip in the ocean perhaps seemed less significant to the human interaction they were gaining in the outdoors, but it was all good, whatever it meant for each person.

Just like the mixing of the sands, the water blended people from all walks of life, culture and class into a community. Some people fell so in love with the new lifestyle that they relocated their lives to be near the water. Now, the hardcore surfers of winter share the empty beaches with equally hardcore dippers and sea swimmers.

Community and unity

At 6 am, I often hear car doors slamming shut in the beach car park. With each slam, an excited person is joining the next as they make their way to the cove.

Sometimes there are two or three swimmers, sometimes as many as 20. My neighbour calls it her "reset". She works in London and when she returns home to the coast at the weekend, she looks forward to her early morning dip. On the calm mornings, giggles and screams of joy from the water travel through the village air. On the stormier days, some of swimmers brave the waves while others sit it out and chat on the rocks. When I was a kid, none of this happened. I've seen pictures of the cove here in the early 1900s, with people in Victorian clothing on the rocks and in the water swimming, but it did not become commonplace again until recent years.

For me, and I think for many others, the simplicity of swimming is the attraction. With other water activities such as surfing, it can feel like there is an endless need for ever-more specific gear, but with swimming, the focus remains very much on the simple ritual of being in the water. Yes, you might need a wetsuit, or fancy a changing robe, but for many, a swimsuit and towel is enough.

It is easy to socialize before, during and after a swim, and for many people the actual swimming seems to be a very small part of the experience. When I swim with friends, we spend much longer talking as we get changed before and after than we spend time in the water. There is a sense of swimming together, and it can be great fun, especially in the surf, but grabbing a coffee, lighting a driftwood fire to warm up, and telling each other about the goings on within our lives is a big part of the experience.

Safety in community

I see swimmers gather before sunrise in winter, and at times just before dark, for a quick dip in the water. For many of us, outdoor swimming is less about physical movement or athleticism, and more about being in the outdoors, and experiencing connection and challenge in ways we maybe don't in other areas of life.

One of the most striking things about outdoor swimmers is the overwhelming women-to-men ratio I notice in my local area. This observation has been echoed by a report in 2021 by outdoorswimmer.com stating that: "The proportion of female swimmers has increased, and women appear to be swimming more frequently than men." It is very obviously something that attracts more women, or is the case in my local area. It is great to see that women are grouping together daily and finding happiness, freedom and security in the water.

My friend Laura and her mum Pat swim together in a large, exposed rock pool at Dunseverick on the Antrim coast. The North Atlantic clashes with the Irish Sea just offshore, pouring pure white surf over the rugged black basalt and into the pool. The pool, with its golden sand bottom, contrasts the wild sea and green rolling hills around it. Laura says: "I like the peace, the calm, the feeling of silk when the water is still and the exhilaration and choppiness when it's not. It makes me feel like I can take on the world because I have been brave enough to get into the sea. I also love the tingly sensation as my skin turns pink when I leave the cold water. It reminds me that I am very much alive!"

Pat echoes Laura's connection: "I love the energy it brings to me, the fact that nothing hurts when I'm in the water. I have arthritis but the water allows me to move freely. I love the group I swim with – we chat, sing, laugh, support each other. I find it life-enhancing! The cold makes me feel brave when I really must dig deep to get out of the house to go swimming. I'm starting my fifth year and can't imagine how I would feel if I had to stop."

Outdoor swimming offers a structured and trusted social circle in a natural setting which, despite the inherent risks, can be a more predictable environment than many urban settings. For women, and men, all round the UK, the water has become a sanctuary, embraced by a community of like-minded individuals seeking a support system that many people may not be able to attain otherwise. A community formed around the water introduces individuals to a network of friends and fellow swimmers with whom they can navigate the dark waters of life.

Soul surfing

"Soul Surfing" is a term used to describe surfers who practice surfing in its purest form; they love the thrill and joy of riding waves and are an underground force of resistance to any perceived threat to surfing. Soul surfers embrace their local spots and guard them from any entity that may attempt to bring a competitive or commercial aspect to it. Us outdoor swimmers can take example from soul surfers to ensure our activity remains free and open to anyone who wishes to swim, without restriction by organizations. As outdoor swimmers it is vital that we protect our ability to swim, to welcome and watch over each other without competition or judgement, and to never allow anyone to divide us into categories.

Unspoken bond

The outdoors can often transcend language. I have travelled the world and experienced many different cultures and languages. As I travel to swim and surf, sometimes language may be a hurdle, but it has never been a barrier to entry when it comes to the sea. I've enjoyed waves with locals and other travellers, despite none of us speaking little more than a word of each other's language. Hand signals to explain where waves are breaking and how the ride was, as well as hooting at each other's rides, are all sufficient ways for surfers to communicate the bare minimum whilst in the water. It is all very primal and simple, and for that reason, the water, and our experiences in them, cut through any language barrier.

There is a huge sense of community around the world among surfers and swimmers, despite many of us not speaking other languages fluently. My friend Pav left Poland in 2008 to live in Ireland. He spoke Polish and a few basic English words that allowed him to get by. He felt hindered by language and so struggled to think of a way to interact and connect with people around him who weren't Polish.

As a lover of the outdoors, Pav decided that he would go to the beach and swim. He hoped it would introduce him to people but without the need to speak fluently in English. He wouldn't need to understand rules or communicate anything other than simple interactions regarding swimming. He met locals and other nationalities, and it transformed his mood, circle of friends, and his life in a new country.

The light of friendship

Night swimming began as a solitary pursuit, one where I loved the escape it brought in the face of one of the darkest times. The release I felt, and the connection I gained to something I already knew so intimately, brought a sense of structure and stability in a time of uncertainty. But over time it has developed into something more, which now involves friends and a wider community.

If you're new to outdoor swimming, always start with small, safe environments, and swim in groups where possible. If you plan to swim in a group, consider having a qualified lifeguard present. Many of my friends are experienced in this field and it brings me great confidence to have them involved. Be sure that everyone in your group is aware of potential hazards. Never underestimate the power of the ocean, and always respect your limits.

Huddled together, against the elements of the outdoors, and also life, we keep an eye on each other. And that is what it is all about, keeping a light on for those in your life, regardless of whether we think they need it or not. We never know if someone is struggling and so we should always be available to those around us for the times that they may need to borrow our light.

Many of my friends and I share the sea as a connection, a conduit through which our friendship grew. Many weeks, months and even years can pass without seeing each other as the currents of life take us to far-flung corners on our individual journeys. But, until such times as we meet again, the bond through the sea remains. And, when we do, we will be soaked in saltwater, immersed in the moment together, enjoying and thriving in the natural world of which we are a part.

No matter what you face in life and how you choose to overcome it, please keep going. Through your struggles you will kindle a flame so bright it will light the way for an infinite number of people.

Keep swimming through the night, and you will create the light.

ABOUT THE AUTHOR

Al Mennie is a modern-day pioneer, adventurer and waterman. Known for his fearless pursuit of the world's biggest waves, Al has pushed the limits of Big Wave Surfing, from Ireland's wild shores to the legendary breaks of Nazaré, Portugal. His surfboard is displayed in the 500-year-old lighthouse at Nazaré, Portugal and other items of his equipment, including a broken helmet, are exhibited in the Ulster Museum, Belfast. Al is credited as being one of "the best big wave surfers of all time" (*The Times*).

Beyond surfing, Al was the first person to cross the Irish Sea by paddleboard between the Giant's Causeway and Islay, Scotland, and his passion for the sea has inspired incredible feats, including a 100-km (62-mile) swim in freezing waters to raise awareness for mental health.

Standing tall at just under 2 metres (6 ft 5 in), Al is also a third-degree black belt, an accomplished writer and a motivational speaker. His books include empowering guides on overcoming fear to deeply personal reflections on loss and resilience. Whether navigating the ocean or life's challenges, Al embodies courage, strength and an enduring commitment to helping others thrive.

ACKNOWLEDGEMENTS

Mark Millar, Leigh Hawthorne, Rich Robinson, Laura Montgomery, Denise Hanna, Youcef Boubetnikh, Jonny Waite, Graham Little, Damien Gallagher, Chris Woodcock, Sara O'Neill, David O'Neill, Tracey Rodgers, Sue Patterson, Charles McQuillan, Vlatko Mitashev, Titus Haug, Sophie Blackman, Emma Patterson, Claire Williamson, Lisa Campbell, Aiken PR, Anne Smyth, Becky Alexander, Marta Sobierajska, Rebecca Black, Simon McIvor, Joe Warden, Daniel Culver, Brian Cross, and Judith Wilson.

REFERENCES

Chapter 2

Kendra Cherry MSEd, verywellmind.com. *The Everything Psychology Book*, Adams Media, 2010

Brent Hogarth, "*Shining light on the dark side of flow-state*" *(#688),* John F Kennedy University, Flow Research Collective, California

Melanie Barratt, "*A blind swimmer's vision*", www.swimoxford.com, July 2022

Chapter 3

Louise Devoy, Curator of Royal Observatory Greenwich, "*Can the moon affect our health*?", www.rmg.co.uk

Chapter 4

Kendra Cherry MSEd, verywellmind.com. *The Everything Psychology Book*, Adams Media, 2010

Alex Lickerman MD, "*Trying new things*", www.psychologytoday.com, April 2010

"*Why immersive learning is the best way to learn a new language*", Robertsonlanguages.com, Wolfestone Holdings Group, Dec 2020

Chapter 5

Oxford Dictionary. www.oed.com. Rip current definition.

Water quality: www.gao.gov/water-quality

Chapter 8

Earth surface water coverage: Water Science School, www.usgs.com, November 13, 2019

Humans about 60 per cent water: Claire Sissons, reviewed Jillian Kubala, MS, *"What is the average percentage of water in the human body?"* www.medicalnewstoday.com, May 2020

Kathleen Holder, *"What are the health benefits of viewing water?"*, www.ucdavis.edu, University of California, Davis, April 21, 2022

Ratih Pangestuti, Kyung-Hoon Shin and Se-Kwon Kim. Editor, Chingfeng Weng. *"Anti-photoaging and potential skin health benefits of seaweeds"*, The National Library of Medicine in the USA, March 2021, www.pmc.ncbi.nlm.nih.gov/articles

#2minutebeachclean campaign, The 2 Minute Foundation, www.2minute.org

#Take3fortheSea campaign, www.take3.org

APPENDIX 1
SWIM JOURNAL

We make many decisions in our lives based on the conditions we observe around us, but feelings and emotions guide us too. And night swimming is just the same.

Keeping a journal of my experiences with the water has been a key part of my learning and connection with it. I often take pictures of the water before, during and after being near or in it, so I can revisit them at another time. I screenshot weather charts, make notes about them, and compare them with previous swimming experiences that had similar weather conditions. I also make a note of how I felt before and after a swim. How I feel before a potential swim is a strong indicator of whether I should be in the water or not.

Here is a simple table listing some of the things that help me make decisions about whether to get into the water, and if so, when and how. This can be adapted to suit your own interactions with the water near you.

Example swim log

Before the swim

Date ....

Time ....

Location ....

Moon phase ....

Weather forecast ....

Tide/flow conditions ....

Observations ....

....

Have I consulted local experts and checked
relevant updates from Coastguard? ....

....

What safety precautions might I take? ....

....

Who will be with me? ....

How am I feeling physically? ....

How am I feeling mentally? ....

Is the water safe? ....

Other notes ....

....

After the swim

Were the conditions as I expected? ....

How I felt in the water ....

How do I feel now? ....

Other notes ....

....

RESOURCES

Water and weather

Global Surf and Wind Forecasts WINDGURU
www.windguru.cz

Global Weather Forecasts WETTERZENTRALE
www.wetterzentrale.de

Global Surf Forecasts STORMSURF www.stormsurf.com

Irish Wave Buoys www.met.ie/forecasts/marine-inland-
lakes/buoys/buoy-locations

UK Wave Buoys www.metoffice.gov.uk/weather/
specialist-forecasts/coast-and-sea/observations

Global Wave Buoys www.ndbc.noaa.gov

UK and Ireland Tide Times www.tidetimes.org.uk

Global Ocean Charts www.admiralty.co.uk/charts

Tidal Atlases www.admiralty.co.uk/publications/
miscellaneous-tidal-publications/admiralty-tidal-
stream-atlases

Pollution Alerts www.sas.org.uk/water-quality/sewage-
pollution-alerts/

Water Quality Updates USA www.epa.gov/waterdata/
hows-my-waterway

UK Flood Warnings www.gov.uk/check-for-flooding.
service.gov.uk/alerts-and-warnings

Weather and Flood Warnings USA www.weather.gov/
dvn/Hazards#RiverFW

Mental health support
Free 24/7 USA www.mentalhealthhotline.org
Free 24/7 UK and Ireland www.samaritans.org/how-we-can-help/contact-samaritan/talk-us-phone/
Mental Health First Aid Course www.aware-ni.org/mental-health-first-aid
24/7 Crisis Line Pieta House www.pieta.ie/how-we-can-help/helpline/

Rescue organizations
UK www.hmcoastguard.uk
USA www.uscg.mil
Ireland www.gov.ie/en/policy-information/eda64a-the-irish-coast-guard/

INDEX

Note: page numbers in **bold** refer to illustrations.